Living in the Gaze of God

Living in the Gaze of God

Supervision and ministerial flourishing

Helen Dixon Cameron

scm press

© Helen Dixon Cameron 2018

Published in 2018 by SCM Press
Editorial office
3rd Floor, Invicta House,
108–114 Golden Lane,
London EC1Y 0TG, UK
www.scmpress.co.uk

SCM Press is an imprint of Hymns Ancient & Modern Ltd
(a registered charity)

Hymns Ancient & Modern® is a registered trademark of
Hymns Ancient & Modern Ltd
13A Hellesdon Park Road, Norwich,
Norfolk NR6 5DR, UK

All rights reserved. No part of this publication may be reproduced,
stored in a retrieval system, or transmitted,
in any form or by any means, electronic, mechanical,
photocopying or otherwise, without the prior permission of
the publisher, SCM Press.

The Author has asserted her right under the Copyright, Designs and
Patents Act 1988 to be identified as the Author of this Work

Scripture quotations are] from the New Revised Standard Version of
the Bible, Anglicized Edition, copyright © 1989, 1995 by the Division
of Christian Education of the National Council of the Churches of
Christ in the USA. Used by permission. All rights reserved.

British Library Cataloguing in Publication data

A catalogue record for this book is available
from the British Library

978-0-334-05650-8

Typeset by Regent Typesetting
Printed and bound by
CPI Group (UK) Ltd

Contents

Preface vii

1. Ministerial Growth and Flourishing 1
2. Supervision and Oversight 29
3. Attentiveness to the Gaze of God 52
4. Attentiveness to the Self and to the Other 75
5. A Supervised Ministry 106

Appendix 116
Acknowledgement of Sources 121
Index of Names and Subjects 123

Preface

I began training for ordained ministry in the Methodist Church as part of the ecumenical community of The Queen's College, Birmingham, in 1986. Within a few years of completing my own initial formation as a minister, I was drawn into the world of Initial Ministerial Formation of others. For almost 30 years I have reflected deeply on the subject of ministerial flourishing and I want to express deep gratitude to the students and staff of the Queen's Foundation, Birmingham, who over many years taught me so much about human and ministerial flourishing. In addition, I want to thank three people in particular who encouraged me to write this book and to believe that if I wrote it, others might want to read it.

My deepest thanks are expressed to my husband Iain who, with our three children, is the foundation and source of all my joyful flourishing. I want also to thank my friend and former colleague the Reverend Canon Dr David Hewlett, Principal of the Queen's Foundation, Birmingham, who taught me so much about shared work, friendship and collaboration and encouraged me to keep developing my ideas about the value and purpose of supervision. Finally, I want to thank the Reverend Canon Gareth J. Powell, the Secretary of the Methodist Conference, who suggested to me that the Church needed to hear something of how we might best enable ministerial flourishing.

This book is an invitation to the Church to consider the role that formal 1-to-1 supervision of ministers can play in enabling ministers and those they serve to flourish. It is not primarily a book about how to supervise, although I have some ideas to share about best practice and how to use supervision most effectively. It is rather a reflection on why supervision might be an effective tool of accountability that will enable us to be a Church faithful to our calling to be salt and light in the world, and keep us on the path to fullness of life. It is written from the perspective of a Methodist presbyter, but I trust much of what I say has value for every person who offers ministry, lay and ordained. Finally, I pay tribute to the work of all those responsible for implementing supervision for ministers and those with significant pastoral responsibilities in the Methodist Church, most particularly the Director of Supervision, the Revd Dr Jane Leach. It is a joy to see the excellence with which this is being achieved.

Helen Dixon Cameron
Easter Day 2018, Launde Abbey

I

Ministerial Growth and Flourishing

Love bade me welcome; yet my soul drew back,
   Guilty of dust and sin. ...
'You must sit down,' says Love, 'and taste my meat.'
   So I did sit and eat.

George Herbert[1]

Houseplants and I have not always been a successful partnership. I know that in order for plants to flourish, the conditions in which they exist must be those that can sustain life and foster potential growth. Plants need the right sort of light, the right soil type and the right quantity of water in order to survive and grow further. If the sources of nourishment are withheld, the plant dies; or if it survives, growth may be stunted and fruits will not be produced. I also know that planting marsh marigolds under a conifer tree is not worth doing – the marsh marigolds relish damp conditions (the clue is in the name) and will die quickly in such arid conditions. I have discovered, by trial and some error, that I can enable the flourishing of orchids – perhaps my efforts are immaterial but I think that I have actually learned enough to help them flourish and I find joy in that. Much attention has been paid in viticulture to the 'terroir' which has been described as the set of all environmental factors that affect a crop of a vine, those unique environment contexts, and farming practices that are such an influence when the crop is grown in a specific habitat. People are much the same as plants in needing the right conditions for stability, growth and development, even if the meeting of physiological needs is just the beginning of human flourishing. Models such as Maslow's 'hierarchy of needs' illustrate the additional need for emotional attachment, affection and belonging as well as basic shelter, food and water in order for human beings to survive, develop healthily and grow and mature fully.[2]

The influences and conditions that create and foster ministerial growth and flourishing are important for the whole Church to consider when reflecting on how ministry can be exercised effectively and faithfully. This chapter explores some of the factors that lead to ministerial growth and development. The subject of ministerial flourishing has always mattered to the Church, not just because human resources are such a core part of the Church's life: being attentive to ministerial flourishing might be even more important now at a time when available ministerial resources are reduced, the numbers of ministerial candidates are reduced and responsibilities and therefore workloads are increasing. The flourishing of all people including ministers is the core business of those who follow Christ, who came that all might know abundant life,[3] and of those who believe that the glory of God is reflected in a living human being.[4] One might reflect that as pressures of workload on ministers are increasing, they are also increasing on workers in the NHS, education and the public services generally. More is being asked of fewer. It might also be important to acknowledge that some commentators suggest we live as a society at a time of heightened fear, uncertainty and anxiety. While this view can be resisted as one that every generation has considered to be true, it is worth taking time to reflect that the Church may be more anxious and fearful than in some other periods of its history. At a time of diminished church attendance there is pressure on a Church seemingly more marginal and less significant in public life to be fruitful and grow and thereby reverse decline. This can make those responsible for leadership at such a time feel they are under pressure 'to keep the show on the road'. So, whatever one considers true about levels of anxiety in society there is clear evidence about ecclesial anxiety, which sometimes results in the setting of meaningless growth targets, performance indicators and impact assessments.

I believe that some of the elements necessary for ministerial growth and flourishing will be internal and personal – such as the character of the minister, their spiritual resources and maturity of faith – and some will be external and extra- and intra-personal – such as the key relationships of the ministry context, and the nature of the context where ministry is to be exercised. For some ministers the context for ministry can be a decisive factor in determining whether they flourish and whether the ministry they offer is effective. For others the specific context is less relevant and they adapt over time to its distinctiveness and particularity, but good quality and healthy key relationships are the deciding factor. What is important for all is the identification of contexts and relationships that are harmful, and which should not be accommodated because they are ultimately unhealthy or abusive.

It is also necessary to acknowledge that some of the most significant experiences that form us as human beings and ministers, and produce deep learning, growth and resilient strength leading to fruitful lives and ministry, may be the more painful, contested and difficult experiences we have. The movement from the selection of candidates for public ordained ministry and the subsequent move into initial ministerial formation, and on to the point of ordination and the beginning of public ministry, is rarely a serene, well-ordered and smooth transition along an uninterrupted path. There are more likely than not to be bumps, bogs and sink holes on the road.

One student minister vividly described, in a learning journal, the ministerial formation experience as being like throwing a firework into a cupboard and closing the door. The result can be colourful, explosive, exciting, noisy and expansive; yet such a move can be potentially disruptive and destructive. Spiritual and ministerial maturing can be a costly series of transitions: some abrupt leaps into undoing and unbecoming, the loss of or disrobing of identity, and the shedding of certainties.

Dislocation, as a feature of moving into a new context or set of relationships, can produce learning but not without considerable intentional reflection on the causes and consequences of the disruption.

At times as ministers and human beings we are simply undone and overwhelmed by what we experience. David Ford notably describes the experience of being overwhelmed as the heart being formed and 'the basic event of Christian identity'.[5] For Ford, Jesus is the embodiment of multiple overwhelming in that he is immersed in the River Jordan, driven into the wilderness to be tempted, and announces the Kingdom of God as being the pearl of great price, a welcome beyond anything we could deserve and a feast beyond our greatest desire. He is betrayed and deserted by his friends, tortured and crucified by his oppressors, and on the cross cries out in his abandonment. Looked at through the lens of being overwhelmed the resurrection might be described as the greatest transforming and disorientating overwhelming of all. Ford reminds us that as followers of Christ and those who in baptism have died to the old life and risen to new life in Christ, we are clothed in a new identity shaped by the overwhelming of creation, death, resurrection and the gift of the Holy Spirit.

We are formed as much by pain and difficulty as we are by joy and fulfilment. A friend who has known great sorrow has said:

> Pain is horrible. Pain is always horrible; but it is never idle. Pain works away within us, shaping and moulding us, unbearably at times. And, I have found, pain presents a daily challenge – to choose whether that pain will transform us or destroy us, bit by bit. This is a daily, and on some days even an hourly, choice.[6]

We believe that human beings are made for goodness, that people grow best and flourish most in the provision of stable, positive learning environments and from the encouragement and trust of others. But we know that human beings also learn, are shaped and formed by separation, loss, failure, conflict and contestation. It is too easy to say that such experiences automatically enable flourishing – sometimes they just lead to sadness and sorrow, but I do want to assert that growth and development, transformation, and even flourishing is possible in the face of sorrow and grief if evaluation of, and reflection on, the demanding experience is part of the response to the pain. The wound of the loss and sorrow will always remain in the soul but the landscape of the new world in which the wound still exists can be shaped and enlarged around the wound so that its dominance and prevailing influence is diminished. Resilience can be found and borne in the face of considerable adversity if attention is paid during and at the end of the experience to the nature of key relationships, if frailties and fears are faced and acknowledged, and if there is reflection and self-reflexivity about the experiences faced. To be resilient in life and ministry there is a need for people to have a developed and mature self-worth, self-control and an inner life resourced by a vision of a future which is better and different.

It has also to be stated in this chapter that the re-enacting of conflicts and the confirmation of the durability of conflict and contestation in the ministerial life and local church life is a familiar experience to those in ministry. How we not only survive such experiences, but learn, change and grow and ultimately flourish despite or because of such experiences of protracted conflict and contestation is a key question for understanding how we become resilient ministers, sustain ministry over decades and how we produce and maintain ministerial flourishing for ourselves and others.

I want to suggest that there are a number of key areas to explore in seeking an answer to the question of what might lead to ministerial growth, flourishing, health and well-being, whatever the demands of a particular locus or context for mission and ministry and wherever we are in our spiritual journey and Christian maturity and period of service. These areas for exploration include the capacity for relationality, appropriate and generous use of power and a demonstration of flexibility and creativity (both personal and organizational).

Public ministry can be experienced as isolating and lonely, and sometimes the reality of daily life contrasts rather starkly with an ideal of vocation lived out in community. It might be said that one always has part of one's mind, heart and will switched on and engaging with caring and serving others, even on a rest day when one tries to avoid engaging with those we care for and serve. Such a state of affairs requires of those who are willing to undertake ministry to be able to sustain highly relational existence in contexts that demand the setting of careful boundaries and high levels of self-awareness. It has been suggested that the majority of ordained ministers are introverted personalities, which means that most will need to become socialized introverts in exercising that ministry and developing strategies of rest and restoration from engagement with others. In addition to issues of personality and intra-personal dynamics there is a need, as part of the task of creating Christian community and experiencing it as part of the household of God, for a mature understanding of relational engagement where the exercise of power and authority is a thoughtful one and where Christian character is visible and made available to others.

Power, Authority and Vulnerability

In Mark's Gospel we read a clear call from Jesus to his disciples to offer loving service:

> So Jesus called them and said to them, 'You know that among the Gentiles those whom they recognize as their rulers lord it over them, and their great ones are tyrants over them. But it is not so among you; but whoever wishes to become great among you must be your servant, and whoever wishes to be first among you must be slave of all. For the Son of Man came not to be served but to serve, and to give his life a ransom for many.'[7]

Issues relating to the appropriate use or misuse of power and authority can be deciding factors in whether ministerial growth and flourishing is possible in any context. Power in the human context is the ability to influence the behaviour, thoughts, emotions and attitudes of other people. Scripture leads us to believe that power can be used destructively or in ways that are liberative and which enable the flourishing and growth of others. We are assured that through the promises of God we have become 'participants in the divine nature'[8] and so as God is powerful so human beings too share in God's power through the gift of the Holy Spirit. Jesus in his life and ministry both exercises power in response to human need when invited to do so, but also relinquishes it and lays down power and control when he chooses to do so. Most notably this is expressed beautifully in John's Gospel:

> 'For this reason the Father loves me, because I lay down my life in order to take it up again. No one takes it from me, but I lay it down of my own accord. I have power to lay it down, and I have power to take it up again.'[9]

How inequalities of power in ministerial relationships, between ministers and recipients of their care, and between ministerial and team colleagues are handled can be a significant factor in whether an individual minister flourishes and grows or experiences significant stress and anxiety, burn-out and illness. Power and authority need to be exercised in ways that are appropriate and helpful and enabling for others. It takes courage for those with less power to challenge and confront those who hold greater power in relation to them. The encounter between Jesus and the Syro-Phoenican woman (Matt. 15.21–28) is a good example of what is possible when careful and willing listening from Jesus enables a woman to broaden and deepen his understanding of the call of God on him and his response to the generous love of God, which then leads to healing for her daughter. Inequalities of power between persons are common, especially in terms of organizational structure, but do not necessarily have to be harmful if the inequality is focused through care and respect for the other.

Authority can be understood as legitimated power that is explicit and acknowledged. It can come from the role held in an organization, and ordination clearly confers a particular authority within the life of the Church. Due recognition of legitimately held authority can lead to an increase in the significance or impact that the person with the authority has in terms of attention, neglect, support, approval or disapproval over others. This means that those who hold due authority need to foster imagination, empathy and humility to remain aware of how powerless and vulnerable others may feel, either at significant moments or as a running thread within the relationship. The intentional nurturing of profound and mature levels of self-awareness in senior staff and team leaders is vital in order that there is growth of all, rather than a favoured or preferred few. Rollo May's work[10] on a model or typology of power as being best expressed as a continuum between exploitative power which dominates and integrative power which treats others in the team or organization as equals, is helpful in this consideration of the appropriate use of power and authority in order to enable mutual flourishing. Equally Celia Hahn reminds us helpfully that we all live constantly in the tension between power and vulnerability. We can all, in a moment, swing from feeling strong and in control to feeling vulnerable, and it is important to have a mature non-anxious presence that allows us to acknowledge the moments when we feel vulnerable. Hahn suggests that denial of our vulnerability can consequently put us at great risk of denying our power over others, and she is clear that denying or ignoring the power we have makes us vulnerable to abuses of power and control over others.[11]

We are called to live, as Jesus did, in the liminal space between power and authority and vulnerability and weakness, knowing as Christians that God chose what is weak to shame the strong,[12] and that power is made perfect in weakness.[13]

Conditions for Growth

A vital requirement for ministerial flourishing is honesty and accountability to God and others about what is going well in ministry, key relationships and the rest of life outside of church and ministry and what needs paying attention to. John Wesley would have called this giving 'a strict account'. Self examination with a spiritual director is recommended for all ministers, as is formal structured one-to-one supervision where the formative processes at work in us and our ministry can be examined in the presence of a wise and experienced person and restorative work be done where necessary. Honesty to ourselves and others about our imperfections, our frailties and weaknesses, defaults and predilections is vital if we are to be safe practitioners, safe containers for the pain and suffering of others and if we are to reflect the glory of God at work in us and the world. Failure to be honest, or an inability or unwillingness to change, suggests that our future growth or flourishing may be limited. One of the most important conditions for flourishing as people and ministers is truthfulness about our relationships, our ministry and our selves. The spiritual life, our life with and in God, is based on the transforming power of God at work in us as well as through us. My own entry into ordained ministry from work in the NHS led me to be astounded in the years after ordination that there was no structure, beyond the very early years of ministry, which would allow for a regular (annual at least) review of progress and performance in ministry. In addition there seemed to be no interest in challenging any of my or others' behaviours or practices that were less than helpful in maintaining or improving standards of practice, performance and behaviour among us as a staff team. There was very little opportunity given for feedback on practice or performance either formally or informally. There was no formal one-to-one supervision available and little overt encouragement or requirement for personal and direct accountability. Ministerial Development Reviews should now be a regular and normative part of the life of ordained people but are not always treated with the seriousness and intentionality they deserve. I have always found the statement by Richard Gula[14] that the particular process of learning to inhabit the ordained ministerial life takes time so very helpful. He describes this process as a 'long arc of conversion' and suggests it must be understood as a response to the presence of God in our lives and as those who are in communion with God, and our capacity to reflect that same glory of God to others. Gula is convinced that the incipient habits one takes into ministry largely stay with us and can be fine-tuned – so if we want to produce a gold ring we should at least ensure the candidate has some gold present in their lives before selection. Paul describes the process of transformation, of moving from being self-willed to living by the will of God for us in this way:

> Do not be conformed to this world, but be transformed by the renewing of your minds, so that you may discern what is the will of God – what is good and acceptable and perfect.[15]

The word 'transform' (Greek: metamorphousthe) used in Romans 12:2 is also used in Matthew 17:2 in the account of the transfiguration. As Jesus' physical appearance changes to the gaze of the disciples present, reflecting the glory and mystery of God, so Paul calls us into a process of transformation to reflect God's glory, as our minds, hearts and wills come into an encounter with the living God. This might be described as conformation to Christ and a transformation of our given nature, which is transfigured in order that it might be redeemed for its true purpose.

In *De trinitate* Augustine describes the image of God as residing in the human mind, and specifically in the complex interrelationship between remembering, understanding and willing that makes up our inner life.[16] To be fully human, according to Augustine, is realized only as our minds are turned towards God as the end of our lives and the ground of our being, so that our remembering is pervaded with the awareness of God and God's activity. Our understanding is rooted in and reaches out for the limitless divine wisdom, and our willing is a sharing in the love of God poured into our hearts by the Holy Spirit. In this exploration Augustine is trying to outline the process by which we are 'transformed by the renewing of our minds'. In Augustine's *Confessions* we hear a bearing witness and testimony to the struggle to accept the work of grace in us.[17] We are fragile and multi-layered beings by our created nature, our lives are filled with the destructive urges of sin, there is much that limits and curtails our desire to turn to God and fulfil God's likeness in us. It is a miracle of grace that we cannot control or demand, measure or possess, which achieves in us the deep desire of God that we conform to Christ. The call to remember and be mindful of God and ourselves before God is neither quick nor easy as a process or pattern of becoming; for such mindfulness to be a totality, the will and purpose of God in us must be harnessed through the work of grace in us – in the purpose and activity of the Holy Spirit. Such is the work of personal, spiritual and professional formation that enables those who receive a vocation to ordained ministry ultimately to be capable of exercising it. In this work the process of transformation is not distinct from that transformation of the self that every disciple of Christ is involved in. Such transformation then is the work of every disciple, but for those called to ordained ministry the outcome of the transformation of the self will be made available to others through the Church in a particularly focused and distinctive way, in the expression of a lifelong commitment of ordination and for Methodist presbyters Reception into Full Connexion with the Conference in a covenant relationship of care and service. To receive a vocation or call to ordained ministry is to receive a vocation with a communal dimension – the call is heard within the Church, it is assessed, supported and sustained by the Church and has as its primary purpose to serve the Church in its mission and ministry to the world.

A free response to God's call on us is to make ourselves available to love and serve others. The ordained ministry we inhabit exists solely to bring others into communion with God. If the lives of the ordained do not reflect the glory of God but rather obscure it, or diminish it, then we must pay attention to what those causes of the obscuring or diminishing are, because they do not pertain just to the flourishing of the individual minister but also to the health of the whole body of Christ.

Formation as Maturation

It is a vital question for the Church to discover how best to enable the transformation of women and men preparing for ordination. The development of ministerial character is not an obvious or easy process. Character emerges as our habits and actions receive a focused attention in response to the beliefs, attitudes and images we are offered and influenced by. We might consider that people influence us as much as ideas. Character is always being formed and is a cumulated, distilled and computed response to our past and present experiences and making sense of who we are becoming takes time. My own experience as a previous Director of Methodist Formation within the Queen's Foundation in Birmingham has involved the preparation of Methodist and Anglican ordinands and ministerial candidates for the United Reformed Church, significant numbers of candidates for ministry in Black Pentecostal Churches as well as working with senior leaders from a variety of global contexts. In a period of Initial Ministerial Learning there is clearly a need for formal theological learning and plenty of it, and there is also a need for being formed and shaped in the habitus of ministry practice usually through placements in local Church work and a variety of placements and attachments with other agencies and contexts such as prisons, health centres, hospitals and schools. There is in addition, as we have already mentioned, an over-arching process of formation and transformation of knowing, being and doing that sometimes is smooth and disciplined, occasionally is fast and furious and sometimes can be a time of dislocation and disorientation which can be conflicted and contested between student minister and sponsoring church. Competencies for ordained ministry are defined by the different sponsoring churches – but there are commonalities between denominations in the expectation that candidates for ordained ministry will be able to demonstrate a capacity for spiritual formation and theological literacy, to communicate well, be a team player and display the character, gifts and skills of leadership. These are all important features, but in addition a personal maturing should be the outcome of such a development process. We are called as human beings to grow constantly and continually into maturity, to be present to and interact with a range of life experiences in such a way that, as long as we are alive, we are never finished with the process of becoming more integrated and more whole and our best selves. There is a need to make a commitment to healing and growth, beginning with ourselves, and moving out into the world around us. Doing this interior work then allows us to move outward into the Church and the world as agents of healing, growth and transformation for our communities and churches and societies. Rather than an introspective navel gazing, this invitation to be courageous and look within ourselves at what needs healing, at what unacknowledged motivations and hidden influences we might be carrying, allows us to offer ourselves more completely in the service of being available to others as effective instruments of God's love and God's desire continuously to make all things new. A robust and healthy theology of the Holy Spirit should see the third person of the Trinity as both present in creation and active in constant re-creation both in the world and in those who have received a vocation to represent Christ in the Church and the world.

In the induction period for new students in the Queen's Foundation it was customary to invite new students to reflect on what the process of formation for ordained ministry might include, demand of them, or present to them. A short film clip of a potter throwing a lump of clay on a wheel and turning it into a pot was sometimes shown. These words were read aloud:

> The word that came to Jeremiah from the Lord: 'Come go down to the potter's house, and there I will let you hear my words.' So I went down to the potter's house, and there he was working at his wheel. The vessel he was making of clay was spoiled in the potter's hand, and he reworked it into another vessel, as seemed good to him to do.[18]

Students were invited to reflect on the skill, patience and persistence required on the part of the potter, the investment of time and energy involved in making a pot. There was reflection on the weight and substance (and cost) of the clay, the knowledge that throwing the pot is only a small part of the process of making a useable vessel, the idea that the DNA of the potter was transferred from the hand of the potter to be in and on every pot and that the clay itself enters into the pores of the potter's skin. We explored the notion of risk embedded in creativity and the creative act. There was clearly an exploration within this exercise of the idea that ministerial formation will include both gift and challenge. Ministerial formation requires a willingness and commitment to making the process one which is conducted in grace-filled, supportive and generous yet challenging ways. It is important to reflect on what factors enable this process of formation (whether a pot or a new minister) – and what hinders it. Any answers can only be tentative but they are born out of a conviction that Initial Ministerial Formation and the early years of ministry should not demand *less* of someone than their former professions or contexts might reasonably expect or demand in terms of behaviours and attitudes, values and actions. It may well demand different things – but it must demand something new. It is vital that ordained ministry should not be a refuge from a demanding, conflicted, complex world for those who struggle to live bounded lives available to others. We are in the world and created for service to and for the world – though called not to be of the world.[19] So interventions concerning behaviours, attitudes and practice with those in formation are sometimes necessary, and timing them and defining them is important. Interventions can sometimes be costly when we meet resistance but worthwhile because the ordinands are gift and a precious resource to be guarded and treasured, especially during a period when more clergy are retiring than there are new candidates for ordained ministry.

The part of the process of formation for ordained ministry which begins within the ministerial learning institution and local church has been described by Kenneth Pohly as 'transforming the rough places'.[20] For Pohly the relationship between those being formed and those charged with the formational process is best described as a covenant which invites people to become active participants in the process of formation rather than passive observers or at best occasional actors in an ancient drama. The Church as covenanted community, and we ourselves, as covenanted disciples, are called to accountability, to freedom to try things out but also to the obligation to own up to failure and the need to account for our practice. This covenant is grounded in the life of the Holy Spirit and the means of grace. Ministerial formation is therefore not a code to follow, a recipe or even a predetermined programme but a life to be lived, open with possibility, changing understanding of our identity and personhood grounded and rooted and shaped by prayer. A formational environment provides freedom to us to offer our personhood, ideas and creativity to meet the challenge of our context in our complex multi-cultural and multi-faith world. It allows for infinite possibility but it also calls us to live honestly as we are and who we might become. The framework of formation presumes that change, growth and transformation of our selves and the practice of our ministry is possible, expected and necessary. In this model of formation the agent of change is the Holy Spirit at work in us and the educators become witnesses to change of nature through grace of those they work with. Theological educators charged with forming ministers, those who hold responsibility in our Church structures for candidates and student ministers and those supervising the early years of ministry in the life of the local church, become like Mary at the tomb of the risen Christ, recognizing new life and bearing witness to it. Never has report writing on students, ordinands, curates and probationer ministers seemed so exciting when viewed through this lens – in this model of the oversight of the process of formation, report writing has become truth-telling, gospel-sharing, witnessing to the detailing of the work of God's grace building on nature. This model is richer than a concept of probation or curacy as apprenticeship to a senior minister. It is the activity of God at work in an engagement with the context and a series of relationships with lay and ordained giving a range of models of being and doing which make a probationer or curate a good minister. Equally, such an understanding transforms Ministerial Development Review and one-to-one formal and structured supervision of ministry if the reports issued after a review or supervision are witness statements to change and transformation. Supervision of ministry, as one form of the oversight of ministry, is thus the enabling of testimony and truth-telling.

In July 2017 the General Synod of the Church of England received a paper on the issues of clergy well-being. Keen-eyed Methodist colleagues who value the Covenant between the two Churches noted that the paper made no reference to that particular Covenant or to the 200-year-old notion of the covenantal relationship with the Conference which all Methodist presbyters and deacons are bound by and supported by, preferring to reference the Military Covenant between soldiers and the crown. The paper proposed that:

In the light of the varying scope, quality and coverage of provision, the House of Clergy wishes to invite the Synod, for the good of its clergy and therefore the whole Church of England, to commit to some form of benchmark in the field of clergy wellbeing. Such a 'benchmark', to which all should at least aspire and be working towards, would be a parallel set of 'expectations' to accompany the set of 'responsibilities' laid out in the *Guidelines for the Professional Conduct of the Clergy*. How best such expectations should be framed to ensure the most positive, tangible outcomes, is an important consideration.[21]

Meanwhile, the Methodist Church continues to work on a draft Code of Conduct for its ministers which seeks to set a similar benchmark and which aims to create clarity on expectations and behaviours. Such codes and benchmarks are thought necessary because many ministers do not flourish and they and the Church need to be attentive to what leads to abundant life, and what behaviours and practices lead away from flourishing, build risk and lead to unsafe practices.

Formational Space and Time

Donald Winnicott makes it clear that a well-developed person needs both boundaries and space.[22] If we are offered no bounds or limits in our experiences or in our relationships we become confused. If we are not given space to grow we will not flourish, we will not achieve maturity but will rather remain infantile in our self-understanding and in our relating to others. We need space and time to play and grow. Formation as play is an interesting idea that merits greater attention and focus than it has sometimes received, particularly in ministerial formation. Other influences on my thinking regarding the nature of formation and the formational experience is the work of Elizabeth Ellsworth[23] who suggests that what really exists are not things once made and complete – but things in the making. Ellsworth has been described as a pedagogical curator most interested in the importance of direct experience and knowledge making, and explores what it might mean to think of pedagogy (the theory and knowledge of learning) not in relation to knowledge as a 'thing made', but to knowledge in the making.

For Ellsworth, things once they are made and completed are dead. So, what insights might be gained from such an idea when considering the process of ministerial formation, growth, sustenance and flourishing? Clearly the process of being formed as ministers is not what can be achieved in the two or three years of Initial Ministerial Formation and Education before entry to first ministerial appointments, but rather all that ministers can learn as life-long learners and learning selves who are part of a learning community and a learning church.

When speaking of knowledge Ellsworth declares that, once it is defined, taught and used as a thing made, it is also dead. Knowledge thus defined becomes nothing more than the decaying corpse of that which has already happened to us. Once fixed, defined and taught, it has already yielded its true nature. It is no longer an organism being formed, continuously evolving through our experience of the world, each other and our own bodies' experience of and participation in that world. If Ellsworth is right this is a fascinating insight into how important the learning spaces or contexts are in the process of becoming lifelong learners and those who are flourishing.

I believe that much of the learning that best helps shape and form our self-understanding and identity comes as a result of our engagement with that which is different from us. Children playing in a park discover that flesh is soft and the surfaces of paths and pavements harder. As children we learn that in falling or colliding we can be hurt – but we can also learn what can take our weight, what can bear us up and allow us to climb beyond our stature to gain a different perspective – the ground from above, for example, on a climbing frame or a tree. Gaining a different perspective or introducing a new narrative can help us to realize the partiality of our own views. Training for ordained ministry only with those who resemble us, agree with us and share our core identity can mean that we do not encounter sufficient difference. Ministers formed in such environments may not be able to enter into dialogue and may only have experience of monoculture. Miroslav Volf explores how cultural conflict encourages us to construct the relationship between the self and the other in a way that is fundamental to our sense of identity.[24] For Volf, a defensive self, unable to integrate its own difficulties into its experiences of the world, is unable to dialogue with or embrace the other. Volf suggests that the self and the other belong together – without the other we can have no sense of the self. Volf suggests we need to embrace and not exclude the other; to be whole we need to receive the other into ourselves and undertake a re-adjustment of who we are in the light of the other's difference. An inability to do this results in exclusion and estrangement. In contrast, a willingness to embrace difference leads to flourishing, health and well-being. Volf describes the development of personhood as requiring generous, flexible boundaries capable of expanding and including that which is other. He suggests that we become who we are in the light of the other's alterity or difference. Such an understanding of personal development lies at the heart of a mature understanding of good formation and raises fascinating questions about the conditions necessary for ministerial health, well-being and flourishing. The research on the variety of protective factors which lead to resilience in people suggest that those who have or are building resilience have good problem-solving skills, are resourceful people. They are able to seek support and assistance from others and are deeply relational, connected to family and friends and a wide range of support structures in community with others.[25]

There is a clear link between the insights gained from Volf's exploration of the benefits of engaging with alterity to a Trinitarian understanding of the nature of God where there is relatedness without sameness or collapse of distinct identity.

In our consideration of the conditions that lead to ministerial flourishing, it is significant that for Volf the formation and negotiation of mature identity always entails the making of some boundaries in the establishment of the self in distinction from the other. It is vital to acknowledge that the unbounded self is as dangerous as the defensive over-boundaried self. In order for flourishing of the person and of the minister to take place, it is the over-guarding against invasion of the other and the assertion of the self over the other we need to avoid.

The work of Donald Winnicott on transitional space, phenomena and objects continues to be important here.[26] He says that for a surprising moment of spontaneous play, creativity, and imaginative putting to use – when we are in transitional space – we are neither our selves as we have come to know them nor are we yet our future other. We are in transition. We are traversing the boundaries between self and other and reconfiguring those boundaries and the meanings we give them. We are entertaining strangeness and playing in difference. We are crossing that important internal boundary that is the line between the person we have been but no longer are and the person we will become.

Winnicott suggests that we should welcome those learning spaces and opportunities that create space for an integration of self and other into a new identity together. Such a suggestion confirms that personal and ministerial formation is essentially communal activity. We are shaped and formed by our companions in ministerial formation and thus our inhabiting of ministry is only limited by the range of practice and attitudes we are exposed to. There is something fundamentally important about the nature of the communities that form us – if risk-taking and boldness, a generosity of spirit and openness to the other are present in the formational community this appears to engender not one example of risk-taking or boldness but risk-taking as acceptable practice. Equally if there is little activity free from leadership based on a command-and-control model, then risk-taking is discouraged and creativity and flexibility will wither and disappear in both the individual and the organization.

In preparing those in initial ministerial learning, the role of the Learning Institution is to create space which is less about finding answers, certainties and solutions and more about the formation of those who know their identity as 'learning selves' and lifelong learners. The emphasis must be more on the process of becoming or extending our capacity as a learner rather than just the nature of learning itself. Matters of curriculum do matter – it matters that ministerial students study biblical languages, Scripture, doctrine and liturgy and hopefully also that attention is paid to inter-faith dialogue and contextual practical theology. However it also matters in the formational process that attention is paid to how we teach, who teaches whom, and when and where we learn. Global classrooms are key in preparing student ministers to live on a big map. Theological literacy must also be accompanied by the nurturing of theological imagination and prophetic action. It is possible that selection of candidates may be the most important step in the formation process. Long before candidates enter the initial ministerial formation programme, their formation of habit, behaviour and character is well advanced. Such formation goes into reverse with difficulty.

Potentiality

The Churches need to ask how we assess the capacity to make the most of a formational experience. How do we discern and identify not just a narrative of vocation to ordained ministry but a supportive narrative of openness and creativity, responsiveness and boldness in order to move from receiving a vocation to being able to exercise it competently as a non-anxious presence available to others? These questions are foundational to arriving at a clearer understanding of how we assess potential for growth and development in candidates at the initial stage but also at subsequent stages of development such as senior leadership. It is not sufficient to search and appoint suitable persons into senior leadership – it is vital that there is a programme of initial induction, support, nurture, challenge and development. Formal supervision and appraisal or development review is an important element in enabling and encouraging development and flourishing, especially in under-represented groups. Failure to provide this structure and tools of attentiveness will result in tokenism of the under-represented group that can lead to a failure to thrive of members of that group. There is a real need to openly acknowledge our failure to be truly transformative in the creation of a diverse Church leadership in which all can participate fully and flourish just as we all participate fully in Christ. Too often in the past ordained white men have assumed that senior leadership is their birthright and territory into which they can welcome and admit others.

Knowing and Being Known

To be fully present to another we must be fully present to ourselves in order that we are able to acknowledge our strengths and weaknesses, our gifts and skills, our vulnerabilities and pressure points before God and one another. Derek Walcott's homage to George Herbert's poem 'Love' is entitled 'Love after Love'.[27] The poem was written in 1971 and offers an insight into the multiple understandings of the self we can have. Walcott, who had both US and Barbadian residency, described himself as having 'one home but two places'. Walcott's poem features a reflected image of the self, not the superficial, shimmering and sunlit image dripping through the fingers as in Caravaggio's depiction of the Roman and Greek myth of Narcissus but rather one which invites a deeper dive, a more intent gaze, a more honest search for the self. Walcott declares in the poem that the time will come for a re-imaging of the self.

The time will come
when, with elation
you will greet yourself arriving
at your own door, in your own mirror
and each will smile at the other's welcome,
and say, sit here. Eat.
You will love again the stranger who was your self.
Give wine. Give bread. Give back your heart
to itself, to the stranger who has loved you
all your life, whom you ignored
for another, who knows you by heart.
Take down the love letters from the bookshelf,
the photographs, the desperate notes,
peel your own image from the mirror.
Sit. Feast on your life.

As I approach 30 years in ordained ministry I have become convinced that only by accepting the multiple and varied perspectives about myself, my behaviours and my practice, which I can hear from those I am in relationship with, can I begin to know myself even a little. I need spiritual direction, supervision and oversight and continuous feedback from others to compare and contrast with the self-knowledge and awareness I have developed over many years. Only then will I be able to have a rounded and accurate assessment of what it is like to be a colleague of mine or be a team member with me.

An Imperfect Self

Peter Fisher in his slim but beautiful exploration of human imperfection *Outside Eden*[28] explores what he describes as the 'unfairness' of Jesus, who chose and favoured the weak and vulnerable precisely because there is for this group of people a knowledge of what strength is given only to those who have known weakness, a knowledge of restoration and new life.

Fisher holds that there is a knowledge given only to those who have known brokenness, a knowledge only the guilty have of freedom – of being forgiven and uplifted and celebrated. It is this knowledge that leads to fullness of life and to becoming fully human. This way of thinking suggests that our own imperfections need to be unhooked from calculation or comparison (I am not as bad as him or her) in order that we can be set free from either cringing before others or wanting to get the better of others. We need to be open to the judgement of God in order that we might know mercy and grace and become part of a community which is encompassed by God's grace and mercy.

Being Encompassed

Denise Levertov, in her poem 'In Whom We Live and Move and Have Our Being', conveys a strong sense of not just being supported and upheld by the love of God but rather being encompassed and enveloped.

> Birds afloat in air's current,
> sacred breath? No, not breath of God,
> it seems, but God
> the air enveloping the whole
> globe of being.
> It's we who breathe, in, out, in, in the sacred,
> leaves astir, our wings
> rising, ruffled – but only the saints
> take flight. We cower
> in cliff-crevice or edge out gingerly
> on branches close to the nest. The wind
> marks the passage of holy ones riding
> that ocean of air. Slowly their wake
> reaches us, rocks us.
> But storms or still,
> numb or poised in attention,

we inhale, exhale, inhale,
encompassed, encompassed.[29]

The Book of Psalms expresses this encompassing love of God as God vigilantly guarding our going out and our coming in,[30] and as God guarding our feet from slipping. In the psalms we learn that God watches over us and keeps us from harm but does not remove us from the heat of the day. Rather he is our shade and protection while the heat continues unabated, but life and flourishing are made possible within it. The heat (perhaps the fear) is challenged, changed and becomes bearable. This leads me to ask what is ministry and life like if it is simply bearable and what does it look like if life and ministry are filled with joy and abundance and ministers and the people of God flourish?

In John Chapter 15 we read that we must abide in, be in relationship with Jesus who is the true vine, and bear much fruit. This Gospel leads us to conclude that our fruitfulness surely is less concerned with the number of new disciples made, on our burgeoning skill sets and further qualifications and more on our virtue, our relationship with God and one another, and our character as those who can love and be loved. While being fruitful can be a reference to the Christian lifestyle in general, I think that something more particular and focused might be referred to in this passage. I think what is being emphasized here is a call to be fruitful in the act of loving one another as God loves us. We are called to abide in God as Christ abides in us and to create, through our loving service, loving communities – we are called to love as God loves. It is our relationship with Christ that enables us to put on love, be love and bear love. The fundamental part of Christian identity is to take on Christ's relationships with our neighbours and share in them with him.

In living and ministering this way we are becoming our deepest and truest selves for we are living (and loving) the world aright.

In Ivan Goncharov's novel *Oblomov*[31] the main character, when asked what he does, replies,

'What do I do? What do I do?'

This is a good question for a man who spends the first 30 pages of the novel thinking about getting out of bed.

'Why,' Oblomov replies, 'I am in love with Olga.'

He doesn't answer the question he was asked but rather the question he thinks is the more important – who are you, and who do you love? His answer is actually a very sharp and significant answer in the novel which is set at a time of a rigidly ordered and hierarchical society where a person's worth is established by their rank, their money, their status, who they are above, and who is ranked below them. In Goncharov's novel identity is created (at least in part) by relationality rather than utility – who we love, rather than what we do, is what is considered more important. The novel is a study in indolence but also imparts some wisdom concerning how we judge each other.

In Marilynne Robinson's novel *Gilead*[32] there is a scene when John Ames, the elderly pastor, encounters a young couple walking down the street:

> The sun had come up after a heavy rain, and the trees were glistening and very wet. On some impulse, plain exuberance, I suppose, the young fellow jumped up and caught hold of a branch, and a stream of luminous water came pouring down on the two of them. They laughed and took off running. It was a beautiful thing to see. It is easy to believe in such moments that water was made primarily for blessing and not for growing vegetables or washing the dishes. I wished I had paid more attention.[33]

I believe that flourishing, resilience and growing and developing human beings and ministers demands an attentiveness to God, to the self and to relationships with others in order to receive and know the blessing of God.[34] Such attentiveness is achieved through prayer and contemplation and other spiritual disciplines, through engagement with community and the created world and through processes and mechanisms of accountability.

Such processes of accountability will be needed in order that there is an experience of oversight and supervision of ministry which is redemptive, supportive and challenging and which promotes health and well-being in the light of God's self-revelation to ministers as they serve as those who are called to reflect the glory of God and bring life to others in all its fullness.

Notes

1 George Herbert, 2017 (1st edn, 1633), 'Love' (iii), *The Temple*, London: Penguin Random House.

2 Abraham Maslow, 'A Theory of Human Motivation' (originally published in *Psychological Review*, 1943, Vol. 50, pp. 370–96).

3 John 10.10.

4 Attributed to Irenaeus.

5 David F. Ford, 2012, *The Shape of Living*, London: SCM Press.

6 Jill Baker, Vice-Presidential address to the Methodist Conference, 2017, www.methodist.org.uk.

7 Mark 10.42–45.

8 2 Peter 1.4.

9 John 10.17–18.

10 Rollo May, 1997, *Power and Innocence*, 1st edn, London: W. W. Norton & Company.

11 Celia Hahn, 1974, *Patterns of Parish Development*, New York: Seabury Press.

12 1 Corinthians 1.27.

13 2 Corinthians 12.9.

14 Richard Gula, 2010, *Just Ministry,* Mahweh, NJ: Paulist Press, p. 75.

15 Romans 12.2.

16 *The Trinity*, 2012, Books Part 1/ Volume 5 (*The Works of St*

Augustine – A Translation for the 21st Century), London: New City Press.

17 Augustine, 2018, *Confessions*, London: Modern Library Press.

18 Jeremiah 18.1–4.

19 John 17.16.

20 Kenneth Pohly, *Transforming the Rough Places: the ministry of supervision*, 2nd edn, Franklin, Tennessee: Providence House Publisher.

21 General Synod 2072, August 2017, *Clergy Wellbeing: report of a working party*.

22 Madeline Davies, 1991, *Boundaries and Space: An Introduction to the work of D. W. Winnicott*, 2nd edn, London: Routledge.

23 Elizabeth Ellsworth, 2004, *Places of Learning*, Abingdon: Routledge.

24 Miroslav Volf, 1996, *Exclusion and Embrace: A Theological Exploration of Identity, Otherness, and Reconciliation*, Nashville, TN: Abingdon Press.

25 Brene Brown, 2010, *The Gifts of Imperfection*, Center City, MN: Hazelden Publishing.

26 D. W. Winnicott, 1951, *Transitional Objects and Transitional Phenomena*, in *The Collected Works of D. W. Winnicott*, Volume 3, 1946–1951, ed. Lesley Caldwell & Helen Taylor Robinson, Oxford: Oxford University Press.

27 Derek Walcott, 1987, *Collected Poems 1948–84*, New York: Farrar, Straus and Giroux.

28 Peter Fisher, 2009, *Outside Eden: finding hope in an imperfect world*, London: SPCK.

29 Denise Levertov, 2002, *Selected Poems*, p. 194, New York: James Laughlin.

30 Psalm 121.

31 Ivan Goncharov, 2014, *Oblomov*, transl. Stephen Pearl, Richmond: Alma Classics.

32 Marilynne Robinson, 2006, *Gilead*, 2nd edn, London: Virago.

33 Robinson, p. 20.

34 See Jane Leach, 'Pastoral Theology as Attention', *Contact*, Vol 153, No 1 and Jane Leach and Michael Paterson, 2015, *Pastoral Supervision: A Handbook* (2nd edn), London: SCM Press for foundational explorations of the mode of attention as a means of reflection.

2

Supervision and Oversight

'Keep watch over yourselves and over all the flock'

Acts 20.28

'Here we are, you and I, and I hope a third, Christ is in our midst.'

Aelred of Rivaulx

Supervision of ministry is best understood as the formative process of enabling the learning and development of a minister that contributes to appropriate oversight of their practice. Oversight is the means by which the Church remains true and faithful to its calling. For the Methodist Church, which I serve, oversight is a corporate and shared activity undertaken by groups and individuals working on behalf of the Conference, and it is understood as personal, collegial and corporate in nature. Oversight is best understood as a defining expression of a community of love, discipline and accountability. It can involve aspects of 'watching over in love' such as monitoring, discerning, directing, guiding, encouraging and caring. I believe that oversight should always be intentional and focused and never careless or controlling. In order to fulfil the Church's mission most effectively, persons in ministry must be publically and continually illustrative of the Church's fundamental dependence on Jesus Christ. The ordained minister should be convincingly capable of offering loving service (*diakonia*) and demonstrate the capacity to be lovingly served by others in return. At ordination authority is given to representatively selected persons to hold responsibility for God's people. Such persons are to represent God to the world and the world to God and, with their diverse gifts and graces, be a focus of unity for the Church. Ordination is a gift of the Church in which all share and in which those selected and set apart for the 'special duties' of ordained ministry are given status and privileges within the Church but also have obligations and responsibility to live lives worthy of their calling. For the Methodist Church these obligations are expressed through the covenant relationship with the Conference that all those in Full Connexion with the Conference are bound by. The Methodist Church has described itself as a connexional Church for more than 300 years and connexionalism[1] is fundamental to our understanding of being Church; no expression of oversight, therefore, can be autonomous, self-sufficient or independent of the Conference. Connexionalism is a form of *koinonia*, a way of ordering our shared life so that the life we share in God is made manifest in the visible ordering of our shared life in the church and Kingdom. Originally referring to the inter-connectedness of people and groups, the word has developed significant and theological meaning for Methodists, being elaborated and expressed through hymns, liturgy and the constitution of the Church as well as in the faith and practice of the Methodist people. Connexionalism is a way of being Christian, fundamental to how Methodists understand the Church and what it means specifically to be a Methodist, through an expression of mutuality, interdependence and of belonging to something larger than a local church, and the benefits of sharing resources and experiences, while celebrating diversity and connectedness. In such a polity public accountability is significant and leads to an emphasis on collegial and corporate oversight as well as personal expressions of oversight.

Formal one-to-one supervision of our ministry is one way of demonstrating the collegial and corporate accountability that the Methodist Church requires. Formal one-to-one supervision has become expected activity for Methodist ministers and is an inquiry into our practice. It is designed to be a compassionate and appreciative inquiry, in a safe and trusted space with a skilled and experienced person, into our ministerial practice and well-being. In formal one-to-one supervision we are able to reflect on and rewrite the stories of our own ministerial practice, because supervision, even if for a brief period, interrupts our practice long enough to permit us to question what has been happening in terms of events and processes and pause for a while, allowing us to take stock in the presence of another, to gain fresh perspective and to review what we are doing and why we thought it worthwhile activity. Supervision can wake us up to what we are doing. When we are in a state of raised consciousness and alive to what we are doing and being, we wake up to what is, instead of falling asleep in the comfort stories of how we have always done things or how we always imagined they should be done. Supervision with a trained and resourced supervisor can offer us a perspective other than our own and enable us to understand more clearly the impact we have on others.

Supervision is therefore a mechanism or process of paying attention in order that we can know and be known, see and be seen, love and be loved. We must be allowed to, encouraged and cajoled into, being surprised by self-knowledge and knowledge of God's activity in our lives and ministry in order not to take refuge in illusion but engage with the truth of what is. It might also be described as recognizing the 'waking life' rather than the dream state we wish we were, or the night terror of who we might become. Patrick Kavanagh encourages us to accept that God must be allowed to surprise us.

> A year ago I fell in love with the functional ward
> Of a chest hospital; square cubicles in a row,
> Plain concrete, wash basins – an art lover's woe,
> Not counting how the fellow in the next bed snored.
> But nothing whatever is by love debarred.
> The common and banal her heart can know.
> The corridor led to a stairway and below

Was the inexhaustible adventure of a gravelled yard.
This is what love does to things: the Rialto Bridge,
The main gate that was bent by a heavy lorry,
The seat at the back of a shed that was a suntrap.
Naming these things is the love-act and its pledges:
For we must record love's mystery without claptrap.
Snatch out of time the passionate transitory.[2]

Supervision is a form of experiential learning where we can name 'the banal and the common' things of ministry and record, and explore with another love's mystery at work in us, and through us, in ways which avoid claptrap, evasion or untruths. Supervision of ministry can be described as reflection-on-action, or indeed, reflection-in-action to result in reflection-for-action. In regular and formal one-to-one supervision, in the present, we consider and reflect on the past events and practices of ministry of the previous four or five weeks in order to gain knowledge with which we can influence and transform our future practice and behaviours. The processes of reflection that occur in supervision can be vital where learning from the experience and practice of ministry can be unexpected and unpredictable. A familiar routine produces an unexpected result we have not seen before. Such an experience, pleasant or unpleasant, contains an element of surprise. Donald Schon is clear that in an attempt to preserve the constancy of our knowing-in-action we may respond by ignoring or dismissing the surprise unless we are encouraged to look more carefully.[3] Supervision is an opportunity to explore the surprise and the disruption it causes to self-knowledge and knowledge of others in proximal and significant relationships. Donald Schon also speaks of reflection after the event which looks back and reviews actions and reflection-in-action, where reflection can take place in the middle of activity, where action can be transformed by the deep reflection taking place in parallel. I have described supervision as being like learning to slow waltz with a partner when we become aware of another who moves with us through the space we occupy but who sees another view. Formal supervision of ministry that is frequent, regular and structured can provide space for both of these two types of reflection on action.

The model I commend in training in supervision skills and practice for supervisors and supervisees is a shared-agenda model where the supervisee brings a number of items to discuss from their ministry practice and the supervisor may bring items too. This understanding of how to use the supervisory space and time gives a sense of shared ownership, shared responsibility for preparation and sharing of the space. This kind of approach prevents either supervisor or supervisee from dominating the space and time – it requires sharing of space, careful listening and attentiveness to the supervisory relationship itself. It promises partnership in the supervisory task.

Supervision as Being Formed/Being Brought to Birth and the Supervisor as Midwife

Frances Ward[4] describes a model of supervision in which she seeks to avoid the suspicions and what she describes as the negativity attached to the 'being watched' connotations of supervision as sight or oversight. Instead she promotes an understanding of supervision as a space to play freely and imaginatively with ideas and creativity. She clearly builds on the work of Donald Winnicott where he describes the importance of creating enough safe spaces for essential growth and learning for children. In this model the supervisor becomes both a safe container that can hold the shared confidences of the supervisee and a playmate who is imaginative and creative in the exploration of what might be possible or tried out in experimentation and improvization. Ward also draws on the work of philosophers Emmanuel Levinas and Julia Kristeva to emphasize the importance of both the supervisor and supervisee being aware of the importance and significance of difference and the stranger within each of them. Ward stresses the need for the supervisor to be authentically himself or herself and yet able to encourage the 'otherness' of the supervisee, so that genuine interplay of understanding and knowledge is possible.

The weakness of such a model for the formal one-to-one supervision offered by the Church within public ministry is that the kind of 'elective supervision' she describes ignores the network of relationships of ecclesial oversight and the responsibilities of the Church. For the Methodist Church this includes the responsibility of the Conference for ministers who are 'in full connexion' with it. The insights gained from it and the strength of the supervision model proposed by Ward, is that it invites and stimulates us to consider how we learn; it alerts us to the need for self-awareness of different learning styles, personality types, and the impact of gendered experience, for example, and for this reason alone is worthy of study.

Just as Ward's model of supervision is about the finding of ministerial identity through playing with ideas in a safe space, so I would want to propose a model of supervision which can include a perspective on the 'bringing to birth' of a public and representative and accountable ministry. This model identifies clearly the transformation of the person giving birth to a new identity and those who stay alongside, keeping the person giving birth and the new life brought into being, equally safe and well.

The shift from an awareness of the self as private and personal to an expression of oneself as also a public and representative person begins to develop within the formation and training period for ordained ministry. But it only fully emerges when a probationer minister (or curate) enters their first appointment. Such a time of emerging into a new public ministry is a time of vulnerability, opportunity and risk, and it is vital that the process is actively and intentionally accompanied. Neil Burgess recognized the opportunities and the potential perils of this period in his aptly named exploration of the early years of ministry, *Into Deep Waters*.[5] The supervisor as midwife is a model which emphasizes the role of the supervisor in accompanying the minister in the early stages of their public ministry (the root of the word midwife is 'with'). The good midwife stays with the labouring woman in order to reduce risk but does not take over, encourages the woman to stay in control, encourages her to trust her body and interpret what she feels, encourages rest, pushing when necessary and safe to do so. The midwife is guide and accompanist, knows that the new life belongs to those who conceived it and brought it to birth, and does not dictate or control but empowers and enables. It seems obvious but it is still worth saying that the new life, if it resembles anyone, resembles the parents not the midwife. The baby is the creation of the parents, not a carbon copy of the midwife. Health of parent and baby, well-being and human flourishing are the values embodied in good midwifery. My own very treasured memory of the midwife who assisted me in the birth of my first child during a protracted and potentially dangerous labour was her sensitivity and ability to stand in my shoes as it were. Her one action that I have never forgotten was her handing me my glasses after the birth so that I could see my son clearly. In this action, in this moment of awareness on her part she enabled my vision. This is precisely what a good supervisor does in giving us from their perspective a new way of seeing and a focusing on what we are dealing with in our ministerial practice. Such supervision then gives us the tools of fresh insight and renewed or revised understanding so that we can return to our practice with a clearer understanding and awareness. Such an understanding of the supervisor as one who shares and accompanies a minister through pain and struggle into a place of new life, growth and flourishing is very rich, and has echoes of the New Testament understanding of oversight as looking over and being with others as a core ministerial task.

I was personally delighted after almost 30 years in ministry to begin a new supervisory relationship in my new role as District Chair, a role of senior leadership in the Church. The move into a new supervisory relationship has involved being accompanied and midwifed into a new role and identity, provided with a safe space for reflection, and a discovery of deep joy for supervisee and supervisor as we recognize and appreciate the reflective abilities of each other.

The best supervision should encourage the development in the supervisee of a capacity for self-supervision in the form of mature reflection between formal one-to-one supervision sessions, never as a substitute for formal supervision with a supervisor but as a developing skill to draw on in between formal supervision. The questions a supervisor might ask in a formal session become the questions the supervisee starts to ask for themselves in the midst of their practice. Good supervision encourages independence not dependence, through self-review, self-monitoring and accountability to the self – the acquisition of this skill and developed practice in any practitioner maximizes growth, maturation and transformation, and is a sign of flourishing. If someone had this skill and then loses it, if they stop seeing what they really know to be true, it is an indication that all is not well and that an external intervention may be required.

Supervision and Oversight: The Supervisor as Overseer

Public and representative ministers should be accountable to God, the Church, their significant others and themselves. We call this corporate and personal integrity. An overseer is 'one who watches over and directs the work of others'. To oversee is to supervise or superintend. In the New Testament the elder or presbyter is mentioned in Acts 11.30, 15.22 and 14.23. Early church governance is thought to have been a collegiate system, with the office of bishop being differentiated from that of presbyter in the second century. In Methodist understanding, the Superintendent minister is charged by the Methodist Conference to share the task of overseeing the probationary period of the presbyter and deacon stationed within the circuit. Those who charge others with this work are also obliged to provide resources and training for this work. This model can contain some elements of mutuality but clearly makes responsibility for, and accountability to, others a key theme. The model calls for collegiality, oversight and friendliness to be balanced carefully and to support and enhance both partners in a supervisory and oversight role – and not detract or confuse. In this model the supervisor as overseer is entrusted with a greater understanding of the context of ministry, the ministerial life, and vision and so carries the greater authority for the oversight task. Power and authority in this context are not equally shared between the overseer and the minister being overseen, and to pretend otherwise is unhelpful and may be a kind of abdication of responsibility. Nurturing a new minister in a new context is immensely rewarding and demanding as the juggling between the idealism of the ordinal and the realism of the ministerial life is managed with care.

Supervision and Transformation: The Supervisor as Witness to Change

Kenneth Pohly, as we have already noted, describes supervision as 'transforming the rough places', and offers a theological model of supervision as covenant committed to life not law. For Pohly this covenant 'invites people to become active participants rather than passive observers or at best occasional actors in an ancient drama'.[6] The Church as covenanted community and ourselves as covenanted disciples are called to mutual accountability, to freedom to try things out but with an accompanying obligation to own up to failure and account for our practice. This covenant is grounded in the life of the Holy Spirit. Such a covenant is not simply a code to follow but rather a life to be lived, open with possibility, change and transformation. It provides freedom to us to offer personality, ideas and creativity to meet the challenge of our contexts. It sees infinite possibilities in our working out how we should minister and where and with whom, but it also correspondingly calls us to live openly as we are and who we might become. The expectation is that change and transformation of us, our behaviours and our practice is possible. In this model the change agent is the Holy Spirit and the supervisor is the witness to the change and transformation in practice and self-understanding in the supervisee. The model calls to mind Mary at the empty tomb learning to recognize the risen Christ and telling others of all that she has seen and heard. To see the task of supervision as that of witnessing to change and transformation in the lives of others and enabling their recognition of growth, maturing and further development is an exciting one. It is an expression of Pohly's conviction that good supervision is not an enabling of ministry – it *is* ministry in its care for another, the placing of another centrally, the attending to the needs of another and the nurturing and supporting function of supervision. It might therefore be considered as a first-order activity in mission and ministry, not a secondary or subsequent activity. This is a point rarely acknowledged as we begin the task of putting supervision in place for all ministers.

Characteristics of Supervision

Kenneth Pohly[7] sees supervision as both ministry and a pastoral event. He defines supervision as a method of doing and reflecting on ministry in which a supervisor and one or more supervisees covenant together to reflect critically on their ministry as a way of growing in self-awareness, ministering competence, theological understanding and Christian commitment. Such a definition assumes implementation of the basic characteristics of supervision which are outlined below:

Supervision is pastoral in function as well as office. There should be giving and receiving of care for both the supervisee and the supervisor. A supervisory relationship can be challenging but should not be destructive or abusive. A supervisor might feel angry or irritated or amazed by what a supervisee reveals or declares but should not, in supervision of another, reveal those emotions by expressing them by raising their voice, for example. Their own supervision, and them becoming a supervisee in that space, is the appropriate location for that exploration of the feelings and emotions evoked within their role as supervisor.

Supervision is a way of doing ministry. We have tended to see supervision as a way of enabling the ministry of another as though supervision is external to ministry itself. I want to suggest that supervision is ministry and is one part of the ministry of oversight. It provides a formal framework or structure for persons to enter into ministry as co-participants and colleagues. It is integral to and formative for effective mission and ministry.

Supervision is covenantal. It occurs within an agreement where persons say to each other: this is what we will do together and for which we will hold each other accountable. This should be a dynamic process that allows for the covenant to be reshaped as needs change and persons grow. Its purpose is to set priorities, establish structure, provide boundaries and identify procedures around which ministry can grow and be evaluated. It is something negotiated together, shared with a third party and agreed.

Supervision is reflective. A particular session of supervision occurs within an ongoing supervisory conversation in which the participants reflect critically on their ministry. While there are identifiable stages through which this conversation flows as the focus of reflection is distilled, the main objective remains helping the participants tell and confront the story of themselves and their ministry as it connects with God's story, as a way of making appropriate faith (action) responses. It is the supervisor's task to help the supervisee(s) see themselves and their ministry more accurately, more clearly and more creatively.

Supervision is intentional. Although the nature of the supervisory relationship cannot be pre-programmed or determined it should have intentionality and focus. There should be at least four growth or development-orientated purposes:

- to help ministers understand themselves, their behaviours and practices more clearly;
- to assist in the development and refinement of ministerial competencies;
- to sharpen and clarify theological and relational (interpersonal) understanding;
- to deepen Christian commitment and focus the practice of mission and ministry.

Supervision should not be haphazard, casual or accidental. Supervision of ministry should have clear goals around the management of risk in relation to the safeguarding of others, especially those vulnerable or at risk even for a temporary period, and the minister themselves. There should be intentional development of well-being and flourishing and developed ministerial practice and should occur with regularity. Six sessions of supervision for 90 minutes in a year may be much more effective than more frequent but shorter sessions or indeed less frequent, longer and reactive sessions because someone is in crisis.

A Shared-Agenda Model of Supervision

Supervision is a guided conversation between two people with the supervisor being responsible for the direction, extent, length and depth of the conversation but open to the input of the supervisee about areas that might be explored. I have described this as a shared-agenda model of supervision. The model suggests that the forming of the supervisory conversation is a shared responsibility. This model encourages the following and makes it possible:

- Neither supervisor nor supervisee can dominate the conversation entirely. In an hour or 90 minutes of supervision, four areas of work are explored; two areas may be the suggestion of the supervisor, and two areas may be suggested by the supervisee. The items suggested by the supervisor are often follow-up matters from previous conversations. This gives the supervisee some freedom and choice while preventing the supervisee from merely 'splurging' and not learning or being challenged or becoming too passive and not learning. The supervisor holds a responsibility to remind the supervisee of items recorded at the last supervision as needing revisiting or further exploration.

- This model demands that both the supervisor and supervisee give time before meeting together to identify and agree their priorities for the conversation. The agenda of the meeting/conversation is shaped between them intentionally and at the beginning of the conversation in an act of distillation. The chance of collision or violation of an expectation is significantly reduced, and it enables the supervisor to reflect on how the key areas for exploration might be focused most effectively.

- This model suits both introverted and extroverted supervisors and supervisees. Each can receive notice of what might be discussed within the conversation and prepare accordingly, and each can be guaranteed being given space. Expectation violations are reduced in this method and careful preparation and reflection time permitted.

- There is a healthy level of exchange and sharing created and being over-controlling and dominating or being manipulated is harder using this model.

- There is a shared sense of responsibility within this model. The supervisee is charged with making the most of supervision, being focused and being willing to listen as well as talk. The supervisor and supervisee must both also actively listen as well as talk. There is a call and response for each from each other and from God within the supervision conversation.

- Supervision occurs within a covenant of attentiveness to God, each other (as supervisor/supervisee) and to both ministry and being-in-Christ.

The necessary reflection on the relationship between accountability and care needs to begin in the place all ministers need constantly to return to, which is the liturgy of ordination[8] contained in the Ordinal. In the liturgy for the ordination of presbyters – after the presbyters have made promises, had hands laid on them and prayers said over them, had bibles presented to them as a sign of the authority committed to them at ordination to preach the word of God and to celebrate the sacraments – the President of the Conference makes this declaration:

> In the name of our Lord Jesus Christ I declare that you have been ordained as presbyters of the one holy, catholic and apostolic Church of Christ.
> Remember your call.
> Declare the good news.
> Celebrate the sacraments.
> Serve the needy.
> Minister to the sick.
> Welcome the stranger.
> Seek the lost.
> Be shepherds to the flock of Christ.
> As you exercise mercy, do not forget justice;
> As you minister discipline, do not forget mercy;
> That when Christ the Chief shepherd comes in glory
> He may count you among his faithful servants.

The Ordinal thus reminds us that the faithful servants of Christ are those who are called and required to exercise justice, mercy and discipline. We don't have to choose between them – they are all ministry. I find that helpful as a concept. Just as helpful is Martin Smith's great sermon for Advent in *Nativities and Passions*,[9] entitled *Let your no be no*, with its reminder that Jesus expected his disciples to say no to some people about some requests. 'No' is not in and of itself a bad, negative and denying word. Smith reminds us that saying no can be as holy as saying yes. Refusal as well as denial has its part to play in life and in ministry. Smith makes the point in the sermon that clearly Jesus expected his disciples to be saying no to some people and some requests:

'Let your word be "Yes, Yes", or "No, No".[10]

So we need to be vigilant that we are not setting up a false dichotomy of discipline and care, and we need to beware of imagining that as ministers we must choose between being caring and being firm and clear. The most caring act for a minister can be to offer a boundary, a limit and accountability to another, and this is certainly true in the context of supervision.

Smith suggests that our reluctance to say no to a person, possibility or an activity, our reluctance to create limits and boundaries, structure and discipline, is deeply embedded in our human sinful natures. Our reluctance to limit or refuse permission, our readiness to accept unreasonable demands and poor behaviours with the pleasing word 'yes' is connected to fear. We like to be liked, to be popular, and we do not like to alienate. We hear condemnation by others if we say no, so too often we give in and say yes.

Saying the word yes is often perceived as sounding the word of actualization by which we open ourselves to a new relationship, to fresh sensation, to acquisition, to building new memories, and to an infinite number of possibilities. In contrast, saying the word 'no' is often mistakenly perceived to be sounding the word of renunciation. It is considered that this word relinquishes and reduces opportunity and creativity, it stifles and limits, it passes options up and it closes opportunities down.

Our reluctance to say no and to create boundaries can sometimes reveal our struggle with limitation of any kind, with finitude and boundaries, a shorter span and restricted space. An advert proudly proclaims that for the product concerned there are 'no boundaries'. It might sound brave and exciting to be unrestricted and unboundaried – but I would suggest it might also be a curse. So I want to suggest that discipline for ministers is a framework that keeps us safe in our limitedness and frailty. Discipline resembles a map that guides and enables us to press on to an agreed or sought destination. Discipline is, above all, a lynch-pin which keeps the wheels on the vehicle of the Church, the vehicle moving and the wheels turning, thus providing movement, travel, infinite possibilities as well as change and transformation. We are released most fully for mission and ministry when we have a discipline and accountability to others. A simple cartoon shows an abandoned car in a car park. The wheels and the engine have been stolen; it is held up on piles of bricks, the car is not going anywhere. Passengers can still climb in, put their seat belts on, put the radio on and pretend they are on a journey – but it is an illusion because without wheels or an engine these passengers are not going anywhere.

I want to illustrate this last point by reference to standing order 700 in the Constitutional Practice and Discipline of the Methodist Church. SO 701 makes the corresponding point for deacons.

> 700 Presbyteral Ministry. (1) Presbyters are ordained to a life-long ministry of word, sacrament and pastoral responsibility in the Church of God which they fulfil in various capacities and to a varying extent throughout their lives.
> (2) By receiving persons into Full Connexion as Methodist

presbyters the Conference enters into a covenant relationship with them in which they are held accountable by the Church in respect of their ministry and Christian discipleship, and are accounted for by the Church in respect of their deployment and the support they require for their ministry.

This is the standing order of the Church which held me safe when I was without appointment following the births of all three of my children. It reminded me that I was still accountable to the Church and was still a public and representative person. I might be at the school gate or changing nappies rather than presiding at Holy Communion or preaching a sermon but I was not a private person. I could not switch off or undo my ordination; I was still, remarkably, a physical embodiment of connexionalism. I might have hoped the Church itself was clearer in its statements and actions than I was about how this connectedness might be expressed on a daily basis. I regret to say it was not, at this point in its history or self-understanding, able to articulate this connexionalism clearly to me, so I had to find ways myself to ensure that I expressed it. So our discipline is vital to our self-understanding as presbyters, to being Methodist people and to our contribution as Methodists to understandings of the fidelity and unity of the universal Church. Our constitution and discipline forms us and makes us, as it reminds us that the covenant relationship, which exists between the ordained and the Conference, is, like ordination, lifelong. SO 700,[11] along with clause 4 of the Deed of Union,[12] are expressions of the foundations of the relationship existing between the Methodist Church and every ordained person. The Supreme Court recognized this and in its judgement in the case of *The President of the Methodist Conference v. Preston*[13] confirmed the key notion that our polity as a Methodist Church is embodied theology (in these instruments is our understanding of the nature of ministry) and our embodied ecclesiology (this is what we understand the Church to be) and that ministers are not employees.

SO 700 reminds us that the relationship between the ordained and the Conference is mutual but the duties that follow are not consensual. We are sent by the Conference to the mission and ministry of the circuits or other kinds of appointments. Ordained ministry in Methodism is a vocation, a call to submit to the authority and discipline of the Church expressed in the Conference, for the whole of one's life. In 1766 John Wesley wrote as follows in the Minutes of the Conference:

> Being in connexion is a power of admitting into and excluding from the societies under my care; of choosing and removing stewards, of receiving or not receiving helpers; of appointing them when, where or how to help me; and of desiring any of them to meet me, when I see good.

The means of connectedness, faithfulness to the vision and unity of the Methodist people which was originally found in the relationship between members of the societies, stewards, helpers and preachers with John Wesley himself, is now found in the relationship of ministers with the Conference and made real to us in and through the standing orders of the Conference. What was for John Wesley an advisory instrument of what to preach, how to preach and how to regulate doctrine is now an expression of corporate oversight of the lay and ordained and of every aspect of Church life including finance and property, mission and ministry.

Our polity is the means by which we fulfil our calling to share what we know as a Methodist Church to be true: that God in Christ died for all, that we are called with others to holy living because there is no such thing as solitary religion. Our life lived in and through God, then, is life lived together with our brothers and sisters.

The Methodist Church needs a disciplined, accountable and focused ordained ministry that responds to the needs, vision and will of God through the Church and not their own personal preference, whim or opinion. In a period of our history when we face a challenge in our use of resources, lower numbers of disciples and worshippers, and fewer numbers of ordained ministers, there is a danger that we are reduced to an understanding of the church which is increasingly one of personalism, localism and congregationalism, often expressed by references to 'my gifting', 'my church' and 'my people'. It is vital that we offer our support and challenge to the ordained to be those who offer bold and loving service in order, that we might draw back from the abyss of too small and limited a vision of God's Kingdom and God's reign.

We are, as a Methodist people, meant to be agile, responsive and disciplined in our offering of loving service to the world. A lynchpin is a mechanism that allows movement and energy to be focused, harnessed and effective. Connexionalism is the lynchpin of Methodism and should prevent individualism and lead to surrender of notions of localism or congregationalism. Pastoral care connects us into a web of relationships because what we offer is Christ's, and we are offering the care in a representative way in order that the love of God is made visible to others.

Finally, a word about the nature of pastoral care. I believe we make a mistake when we think being pastoral is to do with being soft, supportive and kind. The feminist theologian Bonnie Miller-McLemore[14] taught me that pastoral care has greater depth than to offer healing, sustaining, guiding and reconciling to individuals in need, in the terms that the classical definitions[15] have suggested. Rather, pastoral care at its best attends to the web of relationships and systems creating suffering in the world, through ministries of compassionate resistance, empowerment, nurturing and liberation. Pastoral care must be just and generous in its range and should be an invitation to be an agent as well as a subject of care.[16]

Pastoral care is actually a robust practice and discipline – it demands much of us and others, so we should not confuse care with pity. There is a fine novel by Stefan Zweig[17] that explores the consequences of pitying someone without being honest with them. Good pastoral ministry is based on honesty and integrity. Sometimes caring enough about someone is best demonstrated by bothering to demand a change of behaviour, taking time over the placing of limits and boundaries in order to create a safe place for them and others in their care. This kind of intervention can be the highest expression of attention and care. The work of John Heron is interesting in this regard.[18] His framework provides a model for analysing how you offer support with challenge. Heron's model has two basic styles – 'authoritative' and 'facilitative' – which break down further into six categories to describe how people intervene when supporting or being alongside.

Clearly, in supervision we might be more comfortable with more facilitative interventions; nevertheless, if in a relationship that is a means of accountability then authoritative interventions will on occasion be appropriate, particularly around assessment of risk and safeguarding concerns.

Clearly supervision differs from and is not the same as spiritual direction, counselling and/or line management (although some elements of these may be present within supervision). At best, supervision is an inquiry into ministerial practice and thus is one part of effective oversight. Supervision can be a compassionate, supportive and appreciative inquiry into a ministerial life that decreases isolation, provides a framework of accountability and enables growth and development. In supervision ministers can learn to examine and rewrite the stories of their own ministerial practice because supervision interrupts practice regularly and intentionally by providing an opportunity to stop our constant activity and examine in the company of an experienced minister what we are really doing and how we might do it better, and who we might become. Viewed in such terms supervision is a form of experiential learning.

Recording Supervision

Supervision should be regular and recorded. Each formal supervision session should last 60–90 minutes. A record of supervision should be agreed together as the concluding act of the session, signed, issued and retained by supervisor and supervisee and a copy of this record sent to the minister in oversight if this is not the supervisor. Such records of supervision can be useful in helping ministers prepare for the annual Ministerial Development Review (MDR) processes because the supervision records will clearly evidence issues and topics covered in the previous year and reveal issues which reoccur or are absent entirely. Records of supervision should be passed on to the next supervisor when a minister leaves, in order that issues of risk and any safeguarding concerns are passed on. Records of supervision can be drawn on in MDR and could potentially be referred to in competency processes and in complaints and discipline processes.

Management of Risk

The presence of a question on each record of supervision about any issues of risk and safeguarding concern ensures that at each supervision there is the prompt to the supervisor to raise the question of whether the supervisee is currently dealing with any significant safeguarding matter. This ensures that the opportunity is given at each supervision for the supervisee to account for their own safeguarding practice, express any concerns and anxieties about their own or others', practice. Failure to raise their concerns or anxieties when invited to do so cannot be prevented but the refusal to be open and transparent is in itself significant. The record of supervision will evidence any failures to report, inability to reflect within supervision about safeguarding issues and the unwillingness to explore such issues in a safe and accountable manner. A record of supervision can also clearly pose the question of whether any matters which may have been addressed on a number of occasions need a third party referral (to a psychotherapist/counsellor, for example).

Reviewing the supervision reports of the year will allow the supervisor and supervisee to see if there are repeated themes, or indeed topics and issues that have been avoided. Ministerial Development Review (MDR) as a fixed moment in time is richer and more effective when the minister has been in supervision for the previous 12 months, as there may have been considered and mature reflection on some significant themes. When a minister is in supervision and has an annual MDR there is a summative assessment combined with a formative journey which informs and evidences ministerial practice. I have, on occasion, described the MDR annual event as a 'bus stop' moment; the ongoing supervision after the MDR is like getting on a bus from that particular stop and proceeding to journey further. MDR without ongoing supervision does not, of itself, provide a structure for continuing learning and development – although it does provide new knowledge through the seeking of feedback. Supervision and MDR are both necessary and will mutually inform each other but are not substitutes for each other; they are distinct and complementary. The frustration many ministers have expressed about MDR often stems from the failure to follow up issues related within the MDR, thus bringing no resolution or progression. The current position within the Methodist Church is that the supervisor issues an agreed summary report of areas covered in supervision into the MDR process. This brings some objectivity and information as well as a route to allow an MDR to pick up on issues of risk and safeguarding practice.

On a personal note: I still seek spiritual direction regularly but less frequently than when I did during a brief period when I did not receive skilled supervision. I still have specific reflective work to do with a director about my prayer life and developing spiritual disciplines but supervision is giving me a clearer self-understanding and motivations in terms of my ministerial practice. The differences between supervision, appraisal/review and spiritual direction will be addressed more comprehensively in a later chapter.

Notes

1 Report to the Methodist Conference, 2017, *The Gift of Connexionalism*, Faith & Order Committee, www.methodist.org.uk.

2 Patrick Kavanagh, 1972, *Collected Poems*, London: Martin, Brian and O Keeffe Ltd, 1972), p. 153. Used with permission.

3 Donald Schon, 1991, *The Reflective Practitioner: how professionals think in practice*, 2nd edn, Farnham: Ashgate Publishing.

4 Frances Ward, 2005, *Lifelong Learning: Theological Education & Supervision*, London: SCM Press.

5 Neil Burgess, 1993, *Into Deep Waters: Experience of Curates in the Church of England*, Stowmarket: Kevin Mayhew.

6 Pohly, p. 141.

7 Pohly, pp. 107–8.

8 The Ordination of Deacons and the Ordination of Presbyters, *The Methodist Worship Book*, 1999, Trustees for Methodist Church Purposes, Peterborough: Methodist Publishing House.

9 Martin Smith, 2000, *Nativities and Passions: words for transformation*, Cambridge MA: Cowley Publishers.

10 Matthew 5.37, James 5.12.

11 Standing Order 700, 2018, *The Constitutional Practice and Discipline of the Methodist Church*, Vol. 2, London: Methodist Publishing.

12 Clause 4, Deed of Union, 2018, *Constitutional Practice and Discipline*.

13 Ruling of the Supreme Court in the case *The President of the Methodist Conference v. Preston*, 15 May 2013. http://www.supremecourt.gov.uk/decidedcases/docs/UKSC_2012_0015_Judgment.pdf.

14 Bonnie Miller-McLemore, ed., 1998, *A Feminist & Womanist Pastoral Theology*, Nashville, TN: Abingdon Press.

15 William A. Clebsch and Charles R. Jaeckle, 1994, *Pastoral Care in Historical Perspective*, 2nd edn, Lanham, MD: Jason Aronson Publishing.

16 Sheryl Kujawa-holbrook, 2009, *Injustice and the Care of Souls: Taking Oppression Seriously in Pastoral Care*, Minneapolis, MN: Fortress Press.

17 Stefan Zweig, 2013, *Beware of Pity*, transl. Anthea Bell, London: Pushkin Press.

18 John Heron, 2012, *Intervening in Human Relations: An Introduction to John Heron's Six Category Intervention Analysis*, 2nd edn, Leeds: Oasis Press.

3

Attentiveness to the Gaze of God

Nothing is more essential to prayer than attentiveness.

Evagrius[1]

We cringe from the idea of relinquishing, in any moment, all but one of the infinite possibilities offered by our culture. Plagued by a highly diffused attention, we give ourselves to everything lightly. That is our poverty. In saying yes to everything we attend to nothing. One can only love what one stops to observe.

Belden Lane, The Solace of Fierce Landscapes[2]

Keep looking, keep looking that is what the keen eyed naturalists say – keep looking even when there is nothing much to see. That way your eye learns what's common so when the uncommon appears, your eye will tell you.

Kathleen Jamie, Sightlines

Kathleen Jamie is a Scottish poet and naturalist. I first heard her on BBC Radio 4 reading from her book *Sightlines*[3] – a collection of nature essays interspersed with black-and-white photographs. I was driving in my car when her voice penetrated my concentration and I became so captivated by her words I pulled the car over into a layby so that I could attend fully to what she was describing. She was remembering an episode when she was bird-watching with a friend and observing a large gannetry. She was amused by the strutting behaviour of the young birds and the more mature birds nest-building. She was about to leave when she spotted what she described as a pencil mark on the horizon. She took out her binoculars once more and realized that the mark she could see was spray from the blowhole of an orca, a whale. Later she discovered this is a family group of females with young (known as a pod) and she was so enchanted that she went out that day to see gannets but ended up spotting a group of whales. The essay concludes with the astonishing finding that exactly one year later she spotted the exact same whale (the orca are tagged and monitored) 180 miles away from her first sighting – and was bowled over by the thought of meeting up with the whales again after journeying so differently in the intervening period.

In his poetic reflection on the complementarity of sexuality and spirituality in the Song of Songs,[4] Christos Yannaras speaks of us learning to love the landscapes of others' lives that we have looked at with God. When we surrender to this gaze we surrender to God's purposes and will and we see and are seen afresh.

> In the gaze of the beloved, I suddenly recognize for the first time what a human glance means. Everything we see together, everything we touch together, every beautiful sight, everything we taste is born at that moment, innocent and new. Nothing is external or objective, everything is presence.

Yannaras, a contemporary Greek theologian, has developed a rich and complex metaphysic of relation, stressing that Christian theology sees the human person as purely abstract if cut off from relation with God and others and the material world. In his book of meditations on the Song of Songs he speaks of how love compels us to see things differently. If we fall in love with God, even if for a moment, all the impressions of our world that we have sensed become something greater – a common landscape. If God views this created landscape as beautiful and good, so must we. The world becomes, in Yannaras' vocabulary, a gift of erotic joy; an encounter with something which generates desire beyond utterance or final fulfilment. Such is the impact of sharing in the gaze of the beloved.

Antonio Skarmeta's novel *Il Postino*[5] (the Postman) describes a friendship between Mario the postman who lives in Isla Negra, Chile, and the poet Pablo Neruda who is living in exile. Pablo in his exile in Paris writes to Mario:

> I wanted to send you something other than words ... I want you to take this tape recorder around Isla Negra with you and tape all the sounds you can find. I desperately need something, even if it is only a shadow, from my home. I am not well physically. I miss the sea. I miss the birds. Send me the sounds of my house. Go into the garden and ring the bells. Then go down to the rocks, tape the crashing of the waves. And if you hear the gulls, tape them. And if you hear the silence of the stars, tape it. Paris is beautiful, but it is like a suit two sizes too big for me.

What the poet, the novelist and the theologian are exploring here is our capacity for attentiveness as a mode of engagement with the world, and indeed our capacity to witness to what we see. Belden Lane seems to suggest that in our contemporary world we are increasingly unable to sustain attentiveness in a focused and sustained way, and that we are plagued by a highly diffused attention that is our loss. He claims that our diffused attention results from our conditioning as members of a consumer and consuming society that prevents us from abandoning hope that, with sufficient planning, we might yet be able to do and see everything. To move slowly through the world attending to one thing at a time seems radically subversive. We cringe, so often, from the idea of relinquishing all but one of the infinite possibilities offered by our culture. On public transport as a commuter I was often the only person in my carriage that was reading a paper book. Most other commuters were consulting multiple screens on a variety of electronic devices in an orgy of visual stimulation, multi-tasking and information exchange. We are beginning to realize that this kind of mode of engagement may have an addictive element.

I want to suggest that focused or deep observation is the beginning of attentiveness, and attentiveness is the beginning of faithful witness. We are called to watch over one another in love because God watches over us and enters our world as incarnate and embodied in order to be present to us fully. In the Incarnation we celebrate the mystery that God is folded with us, with all humanity, in time and space, in Christ. This is true in this particular moment, and for all eternity.

The Church as Witness: Attending to the World

The Church exists in order to witness to Christ. It is called from the world to dedicate itself to this witness, and it is called back to the world to show Christ revealed in the world's midst. This is what we are called to be – but often fail to do. The Church can and does fail in its witness, fails to reveal Christ and honour God and thus, on occasion, is a poor witness. The pervading culture of the Church can be a hierarchical, clerical, defensive, opaque and unsafe one for the weak and vulnerable. Those giving evidence to the Independent Inquiry into Child Sexual Abuse (IICSA) on behalf of the Church of England were clear that this was the case in some places and contexts but not always and not in every situation. The Church of England and the Methodist Church have both been clear that culture change was necessary regarding its safeguarding practice. Public statements from both churches have been clear that culture change is required, as is humility and a willingness to address unsafe practices and provide an accountable ministry of the ordained and lay. Many skilled people were working hard to create a different and a more accountable Church.

The Church was called into being as a community of witnesses to Jesus. The Church is founded on the commission to the women at the tomb to go and tell others, the disciples, about Christ's resurrection.[6] It is founded upon Christ's commission in Matthew 28.19–20 to 'go and make disciples of all nations'. It is founded on the Pentecostal commission promised in Acts 1.8, to be Christ's witnesses in 'all Judaea and Samaria, and to the ends of the earth'. And it is called into caring and loving service as Jesus from the cross calls the embryonic Church, in the persons of Mary his mother and John, to care for one another, as recorded in John 19.26–7.

The Church therefore exists for the same purpose that John assigns to his Gospel: to witness to those in and around it so that they 'may come to believe that Jesus is the Messiah, the Son of God, and that through believing [they] may have life in his name' (John 20.31). The church is called to witness to Christ as God's Son, and as the source of true life – life that is abundant, fruitful and flourishing.

Attending as Embodying and Pointing

To be witnesses in this way needs to be a matter of both embodying the love of God within and of pointing to Christ. In the first place, the Church is called to embody Christ-like love, to live out the life of love to which Christ calls all people. The Church is called to be Christ's hands and his feet, to be his wounded yet glorified body, in the public square of the world. It is called to show Christ to the world by being Christ-like.

The Church is also called to point to Christ as the source of life: to point away from itself, including away from its own faltering and fallible embodiment of Christ-likeness, and toward Christ who is the source and norm of that love. The Church is not called to preach itself, but to preach Christ, to preach Christ crucified and Christ arisen, ascended and glorified.

The Church's life should therefore interpret and express its preaching, showing something of what that preaching means when it speaks of Christ's love. But its preaching also interprets its life, and names it as a life on its way, travelling in the wake of its Lord, following at a distance but following where he leads. It is therefore not enough for the Church to worship Christ but we must also willingly follow where he leads. It is a besetting sin of the Church to worship Christ but not follow Christ into any of the locations and neighbourhoods he frequents and is present to.

Attending as Local Experiments in Witness

It is important to acknowledge that the Church's life of witness cannot be a static thing. Rather, this life is found in constantly changing local experiments in witness to Christ, in each challenging and changing location and context in which the Church finds itself and in each generation and dominant cultural context.

It is all very well to talk in grand terms about the Church as witness, as if this witness were something obvious and visible when one takes the whole Church in view, and looks at its life as a single fact. But the Church's witness is always the witness of specific people in specific locations, working out how to be witnesses here and now: how to live here and now as Christians, as people called to be holy, as people called to be Christ-like in particular ways with particular people, using particular language and carrying out particular acts.

Our witness therefore is always local (even if the media of communication available to us now increasingly stretches our understandings of locality or community). It always involves a specific group of people, and is found authentically in their distinct patterns of action and speech and relationship. Our witness always takes place at a specific moment of time. It is always particular; it is always concrete. And it is always changing. It is constantly being reformed, one might say, just as the Church is. Witness is something that particular people at particular times and in particular places try – and sometimes fail at, and try again. There can be, if we are relaxed and not anxious, a playful and creative aspect to the trying out of different approaches and strategies. It would help us as a Church to ask what is the difference between an experiment and a failure when we are seeking to communicate with others about our plans, our hopes and our openness to all that the future might hold.

The Church's witness might be said to consist of constantly changing experiments in witness to Christ in each location in response to the insights of previous experience and knowledge of the context. Peter Mandelson always denied mistaking mushy peas for guacamole in a fish and chip shop in Hartlepool during an election campaign, but as a story about dislocation of the 'metropolitan elite' visiting the North-East during an election campaign, it is treasured as a story by northerners who are used to being marginal and so were amused by the discomfort of those who found it hard to interpret a context and culture they were less familiar with.

Attending through Faithful Improvisation

To put it another way: as disciples, Christians are all called to engage in faithful improvisation in witness, for the sake of the Kingdom. Witness is not a matter of imposing a generalized blueprint or programme that belongs nowhere in particular, but of experimentation in situ. It is a matter of the kind of experimentation or improvisation in which one discovers what works and what does not work primarily by doing it: by trying it out, carrying on, and falling over, and picking oneself up, and trying again. It is playful improvisation when play means meaningful and purposeful thought and behaviour that has patterns to it but no prescribed or predetermined outcomes. Play permits not-knowing; a safe uncertainty where 'yet to be' is a position which can be held with integrity. We have spoken about viewing supervision as play and now we consider play as a mode of ministry and witness.

Witness in every age is a matter of improvisation: of trying things out, risking failure, seeing what can be done with the resources that are actually to hand rather than in some ideal world where we could have whatever resources we needed. It is the kind of experimentation where whatever is borrowed from elsewhere has to be adapted to local circumstances, so that there's no guarantee that the results will be the same here as they were elsewhere. It is the kind of experimentation where the particular strengths and weaknesses of the people involved, the saints on the ground, make all the difference.

In 2011 I was fortunate to visit Sri Lanka. In the weeks before the Conference I was due to attend I visited the north of Sri Lanka. The normalization of a country after a bitter and tragic civil war was beginning but signs of militarization of the Civil War were still present everywhere in the form of roadblocks, the continued presence of shells and restrictions on travel. I visited orphanages and homes for those living with disability where the number of young amputees was shocking and overwhelming. One young minister who was in his early 20s took me along with him when he visited the local police station (formerly an army camp). He had developed a pattern of calling in each week and sharing a meal with the station cook. The young minister was Tamil and the cook Sinhala. I was invited to sit under the shade of a tree and share food with them both – only for three jeeps to come roaring into the compound and for the local police/army senior officers to emerge. My presence was causing some concern. We continued to share the delicious food and discuss the situation in Sri Lanka. I listened carefully, and when the meal was concluded I left after sharing my thanks in the few words of Sinhala I had. I was deeply impressed by the brave and courageous act of this young minister – many similarly aged young men would have been rounded up and killed in the previous years by people wearing very similar uniforms to the men we had shared the meal with. He used his language skills in Sinhala to build relationships over food and so increased understanding and communication. After our visit to the camp we shared Scripture together and prayed and I chose to read Psalm 23 vv. 5 and 6:

> You prepare a table before me
> in the presence of my enemies;
> you anoint my head with oil;
> my cup overflows.
> Surely goodness and mercy shall follow me
> all the days of my life,
> and I shall dwell in the house of the Lord
> my whole life long.

The young minister, despite his anxiety, continued to visit his Sinhala neighbours in the camp and to witness the bold, provocative love of God in Jesus Christ who prepares a feast for us. It was good to be reminded of the Psalmist's conviction that he too knew of a God who loves boldly and provocatively and provides a feast in the presence of our enemies, and that equally astounding truth that we are in the company of goodness and mercy as we journey through difficult and dangerous territory.

Loveday Alexander, Mike Higton[7] and others, including Samuel Wells,[8] have all reminded us that the Church's witness is also witness that is called to show in the particular place we are located at this time; the same truth, the same love, the same Christ, the same Father. It is not simply a matter of improvisation for the sake of improvisation, but of faithful improvisation – of finding out how to say the same thing in a different language, in a different context, to different people. It is about speaking of faith in and through loving actions that are credible, compelling and attractive, not in order to draw others in but rather to ease our ability to live and move and bear witness wherever we go. Witness 'as we go' rather than the imperative 'go and witness'.

Witness and Paying Attention

All our local experiments in witness, our faithful improvisations, live by our capacity for learning. Improvising is something we can learn to do, and then learn to do better. And because we are called to *faithful* improvisation – to witness that truthfully shows people God's saving love in Christ – we are called to learn what we're witnessing to, we are each called to learn to know Christ and his love more deeply. In fact, we have to learn the heart of our faith *more* deeply because we are called to improvise witness to it than we would if we were simply called to repeat it. Repetition can be sustained by rote learning, or by the kind of learning that simply hoovers up and then regurgitates. Higton suggests that improvisation, on the other hand, requires deep learning.[9] It requires the kind of learning where one becomes viscerally familiar with the way one's faith articulates what is connected to what, what depends on what, what can be bent without being broken, and what is brittle. It demands that we learn what we can and can't get away with, what we must cling to and what can be discarded as unhelpful accretion. There is nothing frivolous or careless about trying things out playfully, not being discouraged by failure, being willing to try things out. However, learning for the sake of being equipped for improvisation is deeper learning than learning for the sake of business as usual. So those who will encourage improvisation in others in terms of our witness and service need to be given time for formational and learning processes to become digested and matured and incorporated into ministerial being and character. Any period of initial ministerial formation needs to last long enough for foundations to be laid which can be built on and relied on during a lifelong, sustained ministry of flourishing fruitfulness. The wells deep enough to sustain a lifetime of demanding ministry need to be dug deeply and thoroughly. This is why, on the whole, during a period of fewer ministers available we should not rush the formational period or end it prematurely.

That is one of the reasons why it is deeply appropriate to place the idea of discipleship centre stage in our account of the Church. A 'disciple', in Greek, is a learner, one who learns. Discipleship is a life of learning: learning for the sake of witness. Our learning to be good and effective witnesses must be unceasing, ongoing, never ending. We continue to need to unlearn old ways of witnessing (or trying to witness, or failing to witness), and to learn what a contemporary witness to the world might demand of us here and now. We go on unlearning and learning, being broken and remade, doing and being undone, dying and rising continuously. This is our vocation as a Church – to be learners. Our discipleship, our learning to follow Jesus, takes place on the journey of Jesus to the cross and to the tomb. To learn, therefore, and to be fully attentive to God, is to take up one's cross and die to the old self and old ways.

Attending to Christ

The learning that witness demands requires us to pay deep attention to the Christ to whom we witness – and to God's saving love for us active in Christ. That is why worship stands at the heart of our learning, and reading the Scriptures in the context of worship. Worship is where we learn the vocabulary and grammar of our faith discourse.

We point others to Christ by first pointing ourselves to him by our actions, our service and our worship – by attending to him and focusing on him. To be called to witness is to be called to learn Christ: to see more of him, to learn more deeply what he has done for us and what he demands of us. To learn Christ is to learn his faithfulness and to learn his way of sustaining relationships. Our participation in faithful improvisation is part of this process: we look to Christ from new contexts, in the midst of new relationships, and we see him differently. To speak of Christ in new contexts, to worship faithfully in new contexts, to serve new communities faithfully and lovingly demands great attentiveness of us to the person of Christ and the activity of God which precedes and predates us. Faithful Christian existence and faithful Christian witness entail entering into and inhabiting Christ's relationships. When we read in John's Gospel that a dying Jesus says to Mary his mother,

> 'Woman, here is your son.' Then he said to the disciple, 'Here is your mother.'[10]

we realize that all those who are disciples of Christ are all given Mary as our own, and are all given the beloved disciple, and that we are all invited as an embryonic community to care for one another. The witness we make and are invited to share is that at such a moment Jesus is not just being careful and protective of a vulnerable widow but rather he is being extravagant and generous and seeing those he loves as gift and call. He is inviting them into love not hate, into a future not a painful past, into life not death.

Attending to Other Witnesses

The learning that effective witness demands of us therefore also involves deep attention to the great cloud of witnesses alongside and among whom we now witness. We learn Christ from those who have witnessed to him before us and around us. In fact, we can only understand God's gracious love in Jesus Christ through the witnesses to it that we encounter. We learn God's love through all the ways in which we are shown that love and into which love we are nurtured.

We only learn what God's gracious love in Jesus Christ is by learning how it has been and can be witnessed to, how it has been and can be shown. We only learn what God's gracious love in Jesus Christ is by learning together, by learning from each other how to embody witness to the same reality ourselves. There is no manual to download but there is Scripture, history, experience and tradition treasured by and interpreted by a diverse Church which has and does express itself in diverse ways.

So we study the Bible together, we learn in each other's company to read the Bible, the whole Bible, as witness to God's gracious love in Jesus. We are inspired to witness, enabled to imagine witness, and disciplined in our witness, in encounter with the witnesses who speak in Scripture. We need therefore to be those who are in love with Scripture, critically engaged with Scripture, familiar and literate with Scripture and able to attend to the challenge and revelation of the nature of God we encounter in Scripture.

We also learn from past generations, from their history of experiments in embodied witness to God's gracious love in Jesus Christ in whole series of contexts. Their experiments, like ours, were always fallible, sometimes terrible, occasionally glorious, most often something of a mixture, but they were always experiments in embodied witness to God's gracious love in Jesus Christ, and we are able to learn what our witness might become by sitting at their feet rather than dismissing their contribution. We sometimes say that we stand on the shoulders of giants, expressing that sense of discovering truth by building on previous discoveries. This concept has been traced to the twelfth century, attributed to Bernard of Chartres, and much later attributed to Isaac Newton. We need to be those who, as well as attentive to Scripture, can be attentive to the tradition of the Church in earlier generations, attentive in a way which is willing to gaze on what went before, to honour the core values and be willing to critique, revisit, dismiss and adapt as necessary. So we need to honour the tradition, the rock from which we were hewn, but not be too deferential.

And we will, if we are able, learn from those around us now, who are experimenting in witness for themselves, and so showing us what discipleship looks like from where they are, and who Jesus Christ is for them today if we can remain open and not dismissive if their witness does not look like ours. We learn witness along with them, especially when they witness to aspects of God's gracious love in Jesus that we have forgotten, or never learned to articulate or have failed so far to realize how important those aspects might be for us and for the world we inhabit. The Church in the UK has been revived and transformed by Christians from the global majority but is yet to listen with humility or work in transformative ways to include these Christians in the structures and in senior leadership. The senior leadership of most mainstream denominations in the churches of the UK remains overwhelmingly white and male – and we have no credible account to give of why this is so. We are, I think, back in the territory of a pervasive culture that clings to the wet ashes of what has been a burning fire but which now has lost heat and light. The cellist Stephen Isserlis often quotes Gustav Mahler when he speaks of the dangers of worshipping the dead ashes of tradition when we should be rekindling and then preserving the fire (that is the real tradition) in our bellies.

Attending to Our Situation

The learning that witness demands of us requires something profound of us and that is the offering of deep attention to the situations in which we find ourselves, and in which we are called to witness. Witness is an act of communication, and we always, when we communicate, communicate something *to somebody*. Learning to communicate means we must be attentive to the learning concerning the 'to somebody' as well as the 'something'.

When we think of witness as embodying Christ-like love, this should be obvious. One cannot learn how to love people in general, but only how to love this specific person, these specific people – and no two people can be loved the same way. It is no less true when we think about pointing – about the explicit proclamation that points people away from us, and to Christ. To communicate well, to proclaim well, to point well, will look different in different contexts, in communication with different people.

So learning is necessary to witness. Learning empowers our experiments in witness, our faithful improvisations. And the learning that we need to empower our witness will be particular and situated learning, communal learning, the learning of discipleship, learning the way of the cross and the provocative, reckless way of love.

Skarmata's novel *Il Postino* illustrates powerfully how we must be attentive to context in order to discern the glory and particularity of it. The poet who is exiled in Paris, and desperately missing his tiny island, describes Paris as beautiful but living there as like wearing a suit two sizes too big for him. Paris doesn't fit him because, despite the beauty, it is not home. Thomas Lux, who died early in 2017, offered in his poem 'Refrigerator, 1957'[11] precise descriptions of items in their location in a fridge and through close and tight descriptive detail reveals details of a period in US history, the significance of white goods, the illusion of the American dream and the impact of trans-European migration and dislocation after the Second World War, all through an attentive reflection on a commonly seen item in a kitchen.

Refrigerator, 1957
More like a vault – you pull the handle out
and on the shelves: not a lot,
and what there is (a boiled potato
in a bag, a chicken carcass
under foil) looking dispirited,
drained, mugged. This is not
a place to go in hope or hunger.
But, just to the right of the middle
of the middle door shelf, on fire, a lit-from-within red,

heart red, sexual red, wet neon red,
shining red in their liquid, exotic,
aloof, slumming
in such company: a jar
of maraschino cherries. Three-quarters
full, fiery globes, like strippers
at a church social. Maraschino cherries, maraschino,
the only foreign word I knew. Not once
did I see these cherries employed: not
in a drink, nor on top
of a glob of ice cream,
or just pop one in your mouth. Not once.
The same jar there through an entire
childhood of dull dinners – bald meat,
pocked peas and, see above,
boiled potatoes. Maybe
they came over from the old country,
family heirlooms, or were status symbols
bought with a piece of the first paycheck
from a sweatshop,
which beat the pig farm in Bohemia,
handed down from my grandparents
to my parents
to be someday mine,
then my child's?
They were beautiful
and, if I never ate one,
it was because I knew it might be missed
or because I knew it would not be replaced
and because you do not eat
that which rips your heart with joy.

Ministerial students in their initial ministerial formation learn to pay attention to context, to critique the notion that a form of witness such as an Alpha course, for example, can be delivered in the same way, using the same words, with the same format and achieve the same results in a range of different contexts with different language groups, differing educational backgrounds and different social classes and in areas of affluence and in areas of deprivation, in prison and on an airbase.

Paying attention to the contexts in which we find ourselves is vital. Paying attention to our relationship with God is as important if we are to exercise a public and representative function for the Church. There is a clear connectedness intrinsic to God's creation and who we are created to be in relation to God and each other and what we are created for. We are called to ordained ministry from within the body of Christ to exercise ministry among Christ's followers as we share together in God's mission. Ministry exercised this way for the body of Christ requires that we attend to the nature of the body – and ask who is the body of Christ in this place, who is visibly present, participating and included and who is absent, excluded and marginal in terms of decision-making.

What is within us shapes and forms what we offer as our humanity, our witness as disciples, our ministry and leadership. In formation we must pay attention to the inner landscape of our lives. Our hearts must be reachable and breakable. There can still persist an expectation in ministry that as we gain experience in ministry we will toughen up and have thicker skins – that we will swap heart for head rather than hold both together as we discern and plan.

Some Church leaders, women and men, ask if it is possible to resist this way of thinking and if we might have the courage to stay open and vulnerable to knowing hurt as well as joy. In John's Gospel we read, 'Jesus, knowing that the Father had given all things into his hands, and that he had come from God and was going back to God, got up from the table, took off his outer robe, and tied a towel around himself. Then he poured water into a basin and began to wash the disciples' feet and to wipe them with the towel that was tied around him.'[12]

Jesus kneels at the feet of others intentionally and can serve them when he has claimed his authority as one who knows he is loved and called to do so. His self-knowledge and knowledge of the love of God allows him to be present in loving service to others. The Kingdom of love and grace is ushered in by Jesus who is attentive to the gaze, the loving gaze of God upon the inner landscape of his being. He is laid bare before God – there is no pretence, no arrogance, no barriers of defensiveness and pride, just a simple offering of humble loving service.

Isaac Watts expresses it this way:

> Were the whole realm of nature mine,
> That were a present far too small;
> Love so amazing, so divine,
> Demands my soul, my life, my all.[13]

Being Directed in Attentiveness

I am keen that we pay closer attention now at this point in our reflection on witness and attentiveness to the role of spiritual direction and the commonalities between, and differences from, formal structured supervision. The disciplines are distinct – as we established earlier – but connected, and are both ways of being directed in attentiveness and accountability. Martin Thornton once defined spiritual direction as the application of theology to prayer through personal guidance.[14] For Thornton, spiritual direction is a spiritual discipline which is a means of guiding, building and enabling the relationship between human beings which is given in baptism, continued by grace and forged by prayer, in order that abundant life might be known. In this understanding prayer is our response to the status we are given in Christ through our baptism; it is entry to an eternal realm and the Kingdom of God where all might be redeemed, and it is the sign of our continuing relationship with God. Spiritual direction is a movement forward in our relationship with God and our attentiveness to the gaze of God where the gifts and graces we have received can be cultivated and nurtured. Spiritual direction is concerned with our life in

God and assumes the centrality of prayer to that life in God. Prayer is best understood as loving God so that the divine life can communicate itself to us and through us to the world.

Spiritual direction is designed to be attentive to our prayer life and develop it further; it focuses on us as individuals in our prayer and our establishing spiritual disciplines. Spiritual direction should be regular, disciplined and even clinical – it is not to do with times of crisis per se, but rather it should be a regular discipline that can provide direction and encourage experimentation in prayer. The spiritual director who directed the presbyter to 'give up misery for Lent' had elicited a painful truth in conversation with this particular person – she did not know joy in any part of her life at this time. Traditionally the model of spiritual direction derives from three strands. There is the sense of spiritual director not as soul friend but as physician or doctor of the soul who heals, absolves, restores and maintains spiritual health; thus producing the conditions for growth and development. Another way of understanding spiritual direction is that of the coaching of the athlete to achieve fitness and ultimately to win the race, as in Acts 20.24. The coach need not be a first-class athlete her/himself but does hold knowledge about running, the conditions, technique and keeping a healthy lifestyle, and can discuss these things credibly. Third, the underlying dimension is one of relationality, the spiritual director as one who pays attention to the relationship between the supervisee and God. This aspect of spiritual direction sees the director as one of the family, a domestic figure, and familiar with home and key relationships and as one who knows the whole picture – because each and every aspect of life can impact on our prayer life. In these three strands there is much to draw on – the emphases on spiritual direction as healing and restoration, fitness and exercise and a member of the family who knows us entirely without our public masks.

This then leads us to an interesting comparison with supervision in terms of what is common between them and identification of where the two disciplines diverge.

As stated previously, my understanding of the nature of the supervision of ministry is that of Leach and Paterson, namely 'a relationship between 2 or more disciples who meet together to consider the ministry of one or more of them in an intentional and disciplined way'.[15] Equally, the function of supervision I understand to be three-fold, namely restorative, normative and formative. [16] The restorative function of supervision is to support the supervisee by holding and listening and 'restoring them to themselves'. The normative function of supervision is to do with management and boundary-setting both within the supervisory relationship and within their team or organization. Finally the third leg of the stool, as it were, is the formative function of supervision. The formative function is about helping the supervisee to grow into the vocation they have received.

What we can see clearly are the commonalities between supervision and spiritual direction:

- They are both based on a relationship of trust and honesty
- they are usually 1 to 1 meetings held regularly;
- their purpose and function is to support, challenge and enable growth and development in the supervisee; and
- they are both focused on the enabling of a vocation to be lived out.

What we can also see are the distinctive and significant differences between supervision and spiritual direction. There is overlap between these disciplines but they are not coterminous. After 30 years of formal supervision of my ministry and spiritual direction I find my level of frequency of seeing my spiritual director is about three times each year, but I see my supervisor at least six times a year. There are points of connection and some issues or items or insights are raised in both, but I address different aspects of the topic within the two disciplines. I find it more helpful to keep spiritual direction and supervision as ongoing and related but distinct processes of reflection. I have found that by observing both disciplines I have encountered greater spaciousness in each individual discipline and therefore greater focused attentiveness particularly within spiritual direction, and have noted greater spiritual development as a result. Appraisal or ministerial development review is a third annual discipline in a pattern of accountability and only takes place once each year.

- One usually chooses a spiritual director for oneself and considers carefully if the spiritual director is male or female, from a certain tradition or denomination, lay or ordained, or a member of a religious community. One is usually appointed or allocated a supervisor who is either a minister in oversight or appointed by the organization and who will submit a record of supervision to the minister in oversight. Spiritual direction is therefore a privately arranged relationship based on choice and selection that can be changed to suit. Supervision relationships should not usually be based on personal choice or preference.

- One's spiritual director is usually, although not always, someone who one sees by appointment in a context outside the ministry context. Spiritual directors do not usually observe our work or are in a relationship with us beyond that of spiritual direction. The only accounts of our work that are shared are those we offer and thereby control.

- Spiritual direction addresses the relationship between embodied theology and practice and our life of prayer, whereas supervision is work/ministry focused.

Spiritual direction and supervision are therefore closely connected and both focus on the flourishing of the minister and the ministerial vocation but are distinct, and neither should be used to cover all of the areas that they cover between them. Spiritual direction has a part to play in the watching over one another in love in the way that the Ordination service in the Methodist Church commends, but is a personal tool of accountability rather than an organizational one. Spiritual direction is often viewed as a tool of detached attention – it is not based on personal knowledge of the work or ministry of the individual but rather on calm reflection on reportage. It is significant that many seek a spiritual director from outside of their own denomination in order to secure this detachment and distance.

Appraisal or ministerial development review takes place once each year and is a tool of accountability in the same way as supervision and spiritual direction are. The key function of an MDR is to provide a summative and evaluative assessment, lay down a marker of how one is and how one is performing/practising at one point and time. Notably MDR in the British Methodist Church involves a conversation with a lay and an ordained contributor and the seeking of objective feedback. Supervision is the formative vehicle that allows us to progress and work on parts of our self and our ministry, which we and others have observed. Appraisal and ministry development reviews do look back over past events and performance and do look forward to consider what changes of practice are required or necessary or what new gifts and skills for ministry are being offered and which hopes and goals can be identified and shared. It has been significant that ministerial development review was implemented as an annual requirement in the Methodist Church before much consideration of how to implement the formative supervision processes were made. The most important supervision conversation is the one that follows the annual MDR conversation, in that much has been identified that can then be focused on in supervision and given further consideration. It may be that the format of MDR conversations will need amending in the light of the greater self-knowledge and records of themes/issues covered which emerges from supervision. Certainly preparing for MDR and engaging with reflective questions about what has been most encouraging and most challenging in ministry, the nature of key relationships with others, and hopes and future goals, is easier when one has prepared to reflect on some of these issues within supervision. The records of supervision to be completed at the end of each supervision session provide a body of reflective material that can be sifted and distilled as the annual MDR conversation approaches.

Spiritual direction, supervision and ministerial development review are therefore all equally important, are connected and share some skills and approaches in common but nevertheless are distinct and separate tools of accountability. They are certainly all necessary and each plays their part in the establishing of healthy flourishing of ministers and churches.

Notes

1 Evagrius Ponticus, also called Evagrius the Solitary (345–99 CE), monk and ascetic.

2 Belden Lane, 2007, *The Solace of Fierce Landscapes*, Oxford: Oxford University Press.

3 Kathleen Jamie, 2012, *Sightlines*, London: Sort of Books.

4 Christos Yannaras, 2005, *Variations on the Song of Songs*, transl. Norman Russell, Brookline, MA: Holy Cross Orthodox Press.

5 Antonio Skarmeta, 2008, *Il Postino* (The Postman), transl. Katherine Silver, London: W. W. Norton.

6 Mark 16.7.

7 Loveday Alexander and Mike Higton (eds), 2016, *Faithful Improvisation? Theological Reflections on Church Leadership*, London: Church House Publishing.

8 Samuel Wells, 2004, *Improvisation: The Drama of Christian Ethics*, Grand Rapids, MI: Brazos Press.

9 Mike Higton, 2012, *A Theology of Higher Education*, Oxford: Oxford University Press.

10 John 19.26–7.

11 Thomas Lux, 2014, *Selected Poems*, Hexham: Bloodaxe Books.

12 John 13.3–5.

13 Isaac Watts, *Hymns and Psalms* 180, Peterborough: Methodist Publishing House.

14 Martin Thornton, 1984, *Spiritual Direction*, London: SPCK.

15 Jane Leach and Michael Paterson, 2015, *Pastoral Supervision: A Handbook*, London: SCM Press.

16 Franscesca Inskipp and Brigid Proctor, 1995, *Art, Craft and Tasks of Counselling Supervision: Professional Development for Counsellors, Psychotherapists, Supervisor and Trainers*, Eugene, OR: Cascade Publishing.

4

Attentiveness to the Self and to the Other

A circle of trust consists of relationships that are neither invasive nor evasive. In this space, we neither invade the mystery of another's true self nor evade another's struggles. We stay present to each other without wavering while stifling any impulse to fix each other up. We offer the support in going where each needs to go, and learning what each other needs to learn, at each other's pace and depth.

Parker J. Palmer, A Hidden Wholeness: The Journey Towards an Undivided Life[1]

Being well is not the same as being pain free.

Toni Cade Bambara, The Salt Eaters[2]

As we seek a change of culture in the Church regarding the need for accountability in ministry and for our ministerial practice it seems wise to work to foster a mature and considered self-understanding in all ministers which might encourage a deeper and more profound awareness of their behaviours and attitudes, as well as a clear and mature understanding of their impact on others. Such a self-reflexivity needs to be intentionally nurtured and developed in order that there can be a good self-awareness and a corresponding level of insight into the behaviours and instincts of others. It is always helpful for colleagues and team members, for example, to be aware of the natural default positions that they and their colleagues will adopt at times of tiredness, irritation and when confronted with the unexpected. The work of Meredith Belbin is one helpful tool in providing insight into our capacity to hold and sustain a significant number of diverse team roles for differing lengths of time. Belbin's research shows that when we are tired or experiencing anxiety or irritation we will default into a smaller number of roles and modes of presentation, or even reduce to one dominant mode of behaviour, interaction and attitude.[3] This can mean a presenting to others a more rigid demeanour, a more strident tone or a more negative sounding stance.

Some of the points of connection we can experience between, and divergence from, our ministerial colleagues and team members are due to our differences from each other in terms of personality, preferences and style. Other differences that can exist between colleagues and team members are listed below and have the capacity to influence the construction of the worldview held by an individual. Holding significantly differing worldviews can lead to a gap between colleagues in understanding or agreeing what they may regard as a good outcome in a range of situations. Regular one-to-one supervision can be a safe and well-structured place to explore the ministers' developing self-awareness and awareness of others in terms of their presenting behaviours, and a good means of enabling the gap of understanding and empathy to be bridged in a mature and considered way.

This chapter will also explore these differences and how important it is in the face of these acknowledged differences to live comfortably with them and indeed on a daily basis, to exercise colleagueship and team life together while also being a non-anxious presence. Differing worldviews can lead to some very different understandings between two team members as to what a good outcome might be in any situation, plan or project. It helps therefore to map difference between colleagues in order to take that difference into account in a positive way. This will then lead on to an exploration of the need for ministers to be able to create and maintain boundaries as boundaried people with an understanding of their limits and human frailties.

Establishing Teamwork

It may seem obvious to some, although the lack of attention paid to it by others suggests not to all, that every time a minister is appointed to a new ministry context they are usually beginning to establish new key working relationships with someone, and sometimes many new relationships are being formed with a wider team. Usually their predecessor has left and moved to another post but in other contexts they may still be living in the vicinity. In their departure they have left behind them a certain shaped space based on the sum of their gifts and skills, wisdom, experience, behaviours, attitudes and approach. The new appointee may be similar in some ways to their predecessor, very different, or at least have some fundamental differences – sometimes as obvious as being a different gender, age or ethnicity. The new staff member is not therefore joining and learning to be part of an existing team; rather the new appointee is part of a newly forming team. If this point is not accepted it means that even a well-organized induction will not be enough to handle a transitional period well. There will be a need for time and attention given to allow a new team to form that acknowledges that some of the previous patterns and expectations may need to be amended; continuity may not be possible or wise in a time of radical discontinuity. When the creation of a new team is handled well it is usually marked by open conversation and agreement about what is happening and what being in a liminal space and time of transition both requires of all concerned and may provide for all parties in terms of review and assessment and potential transformation, and an acknowledgement of how demanding and costly living in such a liminal and transition space can be. Part of this team-building process is to acknowledge that there is both loss and gain in the new relationships that make up the new team; birth and death are both present and need acknowledging and engaging with openly. It is significant that the Church often welcomes and inducts effectively and liturgically but has less ease around departures, and rarely has a liturgical form of worship authorized for saying farewell to a minister or team colleague. Failure to acknowledge an ending well just makes the new beginning even harder and leaves unresolved, unexpressed and unacknowledged emotions to fester. All that the Church has learned about grief and bereavement ministry needs to be applied to the ending and the beginning of new appointments and the creation of new teams. This is currently a neglected area in the life of the Church and something that can be a factor in whether a minister flourishes in a new context. The Methodist Church's pattern of stationing a minister to a new circuit staff team, and not to their particular designated appointment, should lead to a strong understanding that a circuit ministerial staff is not just an accidental grouping of ministers who are geographically proximal but rather a ministerial team appointed and called to be such by the direction of the Conference.

The work of James Alison on the intelligence of the victim is pertinent here. He suggests that the disciples' fuller knowledge and understanding of the nature of God encountered in Jesus comes after experiencing the disruptive and disorientating, restorative and reorientating presence of the risen and crucified Christ.[4] Out of this experience of disruption and loss their witness becomes compelling and attractive, and new networks of communion and community are established in the early and growing Church characterized by mutual inclusivity and radical action. Alison concludes that we should not shun or be anxious about disruption because it will give us the deepest learning about God, ourselves and others. I would add that we should not only tolerate disruption but that we should positively develop an understanding of its value and develop resources to explore the impact of disruption and dislocation of moves between ministerial appointments more effectively as a Church. There is also an interesting piece of research outstanding into the experience, motivations and reflections of those ministers who curtail, sometimes repeatedly, the length of their expected ministerial appointment for a wide-ranging set of reasons, some of which are external to them and outside their control, but sometimes for internal and personal volitional reasons.

Difference and the Construction of Worldview

Any gathered group can be asked to map what differences they consider exist between themselves which might lead to them holding different worldviews and different expectations of what a good outcome in any situation might be. Some possible answers are:

- Gender
- Ethnicity
- Age
- Sexuality
- Class
- Educational background
- Previous employment experience
- Significant relationships
- Previous ministry experience (including part-time posts)
- Previous experience of Church (rural/urban, new Christian/life-long believer)
- Political beliefs
- Tradition of the Church (evangelical/catholic)
- Personality type
- Preferred team role (Chair, plant, completer finisher, etc.)
- Learning style

The list produced when working with a group of ministers can sometimes be twice as long as this. The mapping of difference between working colleagues and team members is important in a ministerial team but the purpose in the mapping of difference is in order to be able to celebrate the emergent diversity, be attentive to it and the gifts and insights it will bring to the team; and not because it is assumed that difference should be feared because it always leads automatically to things being difficult, pathological, or concerned with contestation. Self-knowledge and awareness of others is at the heart of what makes a team effective and able to weather difficulties by being truly present to each other. One particular difference that deserves close scrutiny because of its considerable impact on communication and modes of engagement, including the handling of conflict, is that of personality type. Sara Savage and Eolene Boyd-Macmillan explore the differently sized emotional spaces introverts and extroverts will require when working in proximity and how important it is to create appropriate boundaries which give space and time for reflection and considered responses when extroverts and introverts are working partners.[5] They suggest that for healthy relationships to flourish and grow there is a need to nurture our sense of union with one another and our distinctiveness from others. The over-boundaried and defended person can be as difficult to engage with as an under-boundaried and expansive person.

As those committed to display ministerial character we are called to imitate Christ, and the challenge of the call to discipleship in our relationships in ministry is to make Jesus' way of life our own. Christian character demands that we love our neighbour as ourselves and are as present to our neighbours as Christ was to his. This leads to a significant challenge in ministry in that an over-boundaried self can be potentially as damaging in terms of working relationships in a team as an under-boundaried self. The unboundaried person is dangerous because they can fail to protect an inner core of a secure self in their rush to engage with others. The over-boundaried self may not be available or sufficiently present to others. Richard Gula reminds us that 'Professional ministerial relationships are formed by the spirit and vision of Jesus and are ones which are inclusive of all and which exercise a nurturing and liberating power in imitation of God's ways with us through Jesus'.[6] We might call this display of Christian and ministerial character congruence with Christ-likeness, and expect to see in those who exercise public and representative ministry a capacity to offer loving service without the need for public recognition, integrity and honesty in relationships, and generosity to others. Ministerial character and virtue is not as visible in those who lack maturity, are self-seeking (they belittle others publically and repel and distance those who seek relationship) and are unable to exercise self-discipline. A key feature of good quality pastoral relationships in teams and in the life of the local church community is mutuality and interdependence.

The work of John Macmurry is of significance when considering team-building and establishing relationships in communities.[7] Macmurry radically suggests that the morally right action is an action that intends community. He speaks of any act of a person as an expression of their freedom and that if the world is perceived as one action, if we are all interrelated and mutually interdependent then any particular action determines the future, within its own limits, for all persons. This understanding means that every person is responsible to all people for their actions. Every individual together with others is responsible for the future kind of community that is created. In Macmurray's schema, when a negative personal motivation exists towards other persons, action becomes self-defensive and is determined not by the other person but by our fear of them. The fear leads to a withdrawing of relationship and the resulting action is the action of an isolated individual. What is required for hope is trust and care for one another. Fear and isolation prevent the creation of community.

It is a truth, not universally acknowledged, that many ministers are fearful and insecure people and become isolated in order to protect their own self-image and worth. Supervision is one tool of accountability that can reduce that isolation and fear and create a safe space where the quality of relationships with others can be explored with another and reflected on. Teamwork and collaboration in ministry are costly and demanding (it is usually quicker and easier to do things ourselves) but are vital if we are indeed made 'of one another' and we intend taking seriously the ministry of the whole people of God and the call we have in Scripture to be partners with one another in the gospel. I believe that greater attention is required by the Church in order intentionally to create functional ministry teams and the enabling of teamwork, shared work and partnership.

Ministry that Leans Towards Others

In an exploration of collaborative practice where teamwork, shared ministry and common purpose combine in mission and ministry together to further the work of the mission of God in the world, I am drawing upon the excellent work of Stephen Pickard.[8]

I do so conscious of how hard some ministers find it to let go of their autonomy, independence, self-direction and freedom to do 'their own thing', and resist entering into formal supervision for this reason. This attitude requires robust challenge because ordained ministry is a gift and call from the Church and whether one believes that ministry is constitutive of the Church (a Roman Catholic understanding) rather than derivative of it (a Protestant understanding) there is a need for us to articulate a relationship of ministry and Church which is integrative and interwoven. In *Theological Foundations for Collaborative Ministry*, Stephen Pickard suggests we need to refocus our theological attention on baptism as the undergirding principle by which all Christians are called to ministry. He argues for a firmly defined nuance: 'Baptism does not ...

so much bestow a ministerial calling as call someone into the ministerial community of the Church.'[9]

Pickard's thesis is that a Trinitarian framework for examining spiritual gifting and vocational calling draws us into a balance between an episcopal framework for the ordering of ministry, and a Priesthood of all Believers framework for acknowledging the dynamic and diverse spiritual gifting of (for) the Church. He suggests that rediscovering the relational basis for ordained ministry draws us beyond the current tendency towards an ecclesiology driven by managerial institutionalism, just as an emphasis on Trinitarian theology has reoriented our understanding of doctrine and worship.

> 'And there does seem to be a consensus that the clues, if not the answers, to some of the most intractable issues to do with the ministries of the Church lie buried in the riches of a dynamic Christian Trinitarianism.'[10]

Pickard calls for an extending of the application of a relational Trinitarian theology as it has been rediscovered in recent years to both ecclesiology and ministry, and suggests this is a natural step forward for us in our discussions about the nature of ministry.

> My ministry is called forth by the ministries of others. The ministries animate each other. There are no autonomous and self-perpetuating ministries. Our life is not only hid in Christ, but our ministries are hid in Christ and in each other.[11]

I believe that a vibrant and energized ordained ministry will only emerge within the Church if the ministry of the whole people of God is richly resourced in order that it too is vibrant and energized. When the Church is fearful and anxious, candidates for ordained ministry become rarer. In a manner akin to the figures in Rublev's icon, Pickard encourages us to consider our ministries and our orders of ministry leaning in toward each other rather than diverging away from one another. I believe that there is a need to reflect deeply on what Paul is actually suggesting when he calls us to be members of one another. The metaphor of one body with many parts all belonging together breaks down eventually and Paul seems to suggest in addition that differing bodies belong to each other and may have a claim on each other. The suggestion seems to be made that ministries can only be authentic in as much as they relate to one another and are not self-constituting but are constituted both from and toward others and collaborate in the gospel of Jesus Christ. Tom Smail's exploration of the patterns of renewal in the Church, and the need for a mature theological model of the work of the Holy Spirit, led him to emphasize a paschal rather than a Pentecostal model for the gift of the Holy Spirit[12] and we find this model in both John and Paul. John links cross and Spirit; and in John 19.30 Jesus 'hands over the spirit' on the cross – not just his spirit, but the Spirit of Calvary, the same spirit by which he has just defeated the powers of evil. The Spirit doesn't wait for Pentecost. In John 19.34-5 the blood and water flow from Jesus' side; and in John's Gospel water is always the symbol of the Spirit – so to say that water flows from the wounded side of the crucified Jesus is to say that the Spirit comes from the cross. In John's Gospel, the way of the cross and the way of the Spirit are one and the same. There are not two circles, one with cross and one with Spirit at their centres, but only one, with the crucified and risen Lord at the centre. Paul shows this same awareness in 1 Corinthians 1.22: 'Jews demand signs, and Greeks desire wisdom, but we preach Christ crucified.' The Spirit leads us, as he led Jesus, to glory fashioned in suffering, to victory won through defeat, to power exercised in weakness, to a throne that is the same shape as a cross. This Spirit will never lead us away from or past the cross of Christ; rather the Spirit will consistently bring us back to it, because it is the one source of that strange power by which God through Christ has overcome the world. Smail's argument that God, more often than not, desires to lead us through suffering rather than deliver us from it would be more cogent if he stressed that God's desire to lead us through suffering manifests itself in the communion we receive from the Holy Spirit.

The Holy Spirit unites believers with Christ, through whom they experience the communion of the Triune life by participation. Part of this participation is that while we participate in the self-giving communion of the Holy Trinity, we are discovering and establishing communion with others. In the Christian community, therefore, there can be no such thing as a solitary sufferer; for the suffering of one is the suffering of all. The Holy Spirit opens us outwardly to one another and thus we are enabled to wait with, endure with, and witness to those suffering in our midst. Regardless of the shape suffering takes, an anthropology informed by the Trinitarian being-in-relation helps to elucidate the disciple's call to take up their cross – for we do not carry it alone. In his epistle to the Galatians Paul says, 'Bear one another's burdens, and in this way you will fulfil the law of Christ' (Gal. 6.2). When the resurrection community bears the burdens of one another, the act of sharing in or interceding for one who is suffering is already a sign of the Holy Spirit's transformation and 'empowerment'. The *koinonia* fellowship of the Spirit, which is the primary shape of the Church's life together, is most evident in the community's sacrifice, eschewing self-centredness for the sake of the other.

Our loving, at least when it has the form of service, always means our *dispossession*. It always involves our surrendering to another something of our own, something that secures our old identity as self-contained beings. In other words, the spirit of sacrifice in the Spirit-led community is already a sign of the Spirit leading the community *towards* the cross, not away from it. We might summarize this by declaring that God is not doing anything on Good Friday that is uncharacteristic of God. Likewise, when God unites believers to Christ by the Holy Spirit, it will not be uncharacteristic of the resurrection community to endure suffering. For in their communion with the Holy Trinity and consequently with one another, they are witnessing to the power of self-giving love – a power misunderstood by the world and thus deemed threatening. The Spirit that produces fruits for ministry in us is a Spirit given from the cross of Christ; these fruits are openness to dispossession, willingness for surrender and sacrifice, and the capacity for provocative loving. These are the signs we would seek in those whose ministry we long to see flourishing, developing and bearing fruit. Clearly individual ministerial flourishing flows from the presence of flourishing in the Church community. A frail Church might mean ministers struggle to flourish themselves.

Discovering Common Ground

When an elderly Methodist minister was sitting down (retiring from active ministry), speeches were made in appreciation of his 30 years of ordained ministry and his contribution to the Church; the most memorable speech was the one that stated with some awe and wonder: 'Joe worked in team ministry for the whole of his ministry and always discovered some common ground with everyone he worked with.' Team ministry and shared and collaborative practice can be energizing and fun, but can also be dire, dysfunctional and occasionally downright destructive. Inherent and fundamental difference between people is rarely the sole issue, but failing to acknowledge difference and be willing to receive another minister's perspective can lead to tension, aggression and outright hostility at times. Rather than be receptive to another, the prevailing attitude can be to project onto, and then defend against, difference encountered in another. Classically this is the difficulty we face in seeing the other person as a threat to our well-defended and controlled position rather than gift to us. When the group dynamic is factored into the inter-personal and intra-personal dynamic this can lead to a situation of tension unless these dynamics are acknowledged and attended to. Occasional group supervision or external facilitation of a team at times of difficulty can prove helpful in order to keep relationships healthy and open to scrutiny, in addition to an initial mapping of the team in terms of personality and role, needs, perceptions and emotional preference. In increasing the awareness of the group and team about their impact on each other and the varied perspectives they each hold on a particular issue, the capacity of the team to be changed by working together, challenged and supported in healthy ways can be changed. Every group or team is made up of individuals who all have a 'surreptitious agenda' created from inner motivations and forces, not always conscious, that cause us to handle situations in ways that serve our ego more than our context. The intentional creation of mutual trust, respect and dialogue is vital in the creation of a healthy team who can handle conflict without falling apart, or tearing each other apart, and this requires of us attentive listening and quality of presence and the avoidance of command-and-control models of leadership. The establishing of common ground, shared vision and commitment to loving service can allow very different people to find that rather than 'us or me' and 'them' there can be the discovery of 'we' and a commitment to multi-voiced teams who know the power of 'all' and are effective in partnership.

Rowan Williams suggests that intentional work in this area can be life-giving and that we cannot begin to think about life in community as an abstract or theoretical consideration because our life and our death is with our neighbour – if we sin against our neighbour we have sinned against Christ. 'The life of intimacy with God in contemplation is both the fruit and the course of a renewed life together.'[13] Our relationship with eternal love and truth is bound up with how we manage the key relationships of proximity. Every ministry team is a group of persons-in-relation established and mediated through Christ.

Rowan Williams directs us to the insight of Moses the Black[14] who declared, 'The monk must die to his neighbour and never judge him at all in any way whatever.' If our life is with our neighbour then we must take great care about what we are willing to say or think about our neighbour. If we belong together then for both of us our well-being and flourishing is caught up with what we say to or about our neighbour. We must be able to give each other space in which to flourish and our capacity to do this is directly related to our ability to be attentive to each other.

Annie Dillard,[15] who pays glorious and detailed attention to the natural world, suggests that honest self-expression is the hardest thing in the world; it needs self-scrutiny and self-abandonment and we not inclined naturally to either. This leads me to suggest that in order for the flourishing of others to be something we actively contribute to, we might need to be willing to abandon our preconceptions about ourselves, our ministry, including our deepest convictions about what our gifts and graces for ministry actually are, or how others receive them. We will not find this easy because we prefer to cling to illusions and dreams about ourselves. It is in the presence of, and living in, the gaze of God, mediated by another person, that we can discover our core identity. We need to be able to do so confidently without fear and without deceiving others and ourselves. Williams concludes 'without manifestation of thoughts, there is no progress'.[16] The sin of failure is healed by solidarity with others and by identification with them. The power of sin is overcome by the power of the cross, by Christ enduring suffering for our sake. From the cross Christ calls the embryonic Church into existence, and through the gift of Christ from the cross our shared life and our shared ministry together is born.

Attending to ourselves and to our neighbours in ministry is demanding but necessary if we are to grow and flourish and be credible witnesses to the love and grace of God. Our personal growth and flourishing in ministry is dependent on our ability and capacity for establishing the conditions for others to grow and develop; the enabling of the ministry of others is part of our calling. This leads me to consider now in more detail issues around boundary keeping.

Creating Boundaries

The covenantal action of trusting and accepting the trust of others in ministry and ministering to others makes fidelity to trust the fundamental moral imperative for the pastoral minister. In professional ethics this imperative is called the professional's *fiduciary responsibility*.[17] It means that we are called to exercise our power and authority in ways that will serve the needs of others above and before we serve our own. In order to do this we are responsible for maintaining the boundaries of the professional relationship. In order for the pastoral encounter to be about the other person and not us, it becomes our responsibility to make clear boundaries which create a safe space for their experiences to be reflected on without having to pay attention to our needs, desires and conflicts at the same time. We must exercise self-discipline to ensure that we do not use our pastoral relationships to satisfy our desires for attention, acceptance, pleasure, profit, gratification, self-esteem and self-worth. Formal supervision of our ministerial practice is a good opportunity to reflect on potential failures or particular stresses in these areas with another experienced practitioner.

Most pastoral relationships are unequal in terms of power, and usually the minister is the one with most power, and how we exercise that power and authority is key because to trust another and entrust them with knowledge of our being is to become vulnerable to them. Within a ministry team the same dynamic applies. It is therefore vital that we can acknowledge and own the power we have. We are most at risk of unethical behaviour when we minimize or ignore the size of our power. The greater burden of responsibility in any relationship lies with the person with most power. This dynamic clearly applies within ministry teams for team leaders and members of the team and needs to be paid close attention. A helpful feature of any supervisory relationship is a conversation which pays attention to the supervisory relationship itself in terms of its use of power and control, its capacity to enable, challenge and support.

It is important to register that friendship and pastoral relationships are complex matters and not the same. We choose and select our friends; we are usually mutual, equal, kind to each other, reciprocal in knowledge and self-disclosure within our friendships; some of that may be true for the best pastoral relationships. But we are not usually able to choose whom we will minister to or work alongside in a team. There are a range of views expressed about whether friendship and colleagueship is wise or possible, and very few writers suggest that we can never have friends in congregations nor that we can never minister to friends or be ministered to by friends but the dangers of displaying favouritism in congregations and teams should be noted, and friendships are altered when we do go on to offer professional care or develop a working relationship. One lens of interpretation that can be useful is to consider what 'voices' we are used to hearing from our friends – usually the 'voice' we are used to hearing is one of affirmation, encouragement, support and some challenge when invited to offer an opinion. Once the friend becomes a colleague or a colleague also becomes a friend the 'voices' which are used will be multiple and perhaps contradictory or confusing. This can all be negotiated with care, but if the boundaries are not attended to there can be considerable confusion for the two persons concerned but also for others in the same context or team.

The key to negotiating these complexities and dual relationships may be to know when to refer on if we want to keep the friendship or to advise that the friendship needs to end if colleagueship has the greater priority. The demands of ministry or teamworking can conflict with the friendship. We might need to ask:

Which role is dominant for me in this relationship?
Who am I for you in this relationship?
Who are you for me?
Whose needs are being met?
Whose needs are being ignored?

Dual Relationships

When we interact with another person in more than one capacity, we form a dual relationship. At the school gate are we the vicar/pastor/minister or are we Tommy's best friend or John's Mum? If Tommy's Mum and Dad's marriage breaks down, and Tommy's dad goes off with John's friend Emma's Mum and John's Mum is supporting both Tommy's Mum and Emma's Dad, who are all appearing at the school gate some days, her relationship with Emma's Mum becomes complex and open to misinterpretation by all parties.

In smaller communities dual relationships become more likely and harder to avoid. They only become problematic when roles get confused and boundaries are not respected. A good question to ask in terms of the sharing of information is in what role was I when someone told me this information? Clearly married couples enter ministry teams and become working colleagues as well as partners and for other ministry team members and for the persons themselves clarity about confidentiality and inter-personal dynamics is key.

In situations where boundaries are blurred it helps to

- be honest with yourself;
- be honest with others;
- pay attention to your own needs;
- satisfy your needs for support and affirmation beyond this particular relationship;
- keep the pastoral role or team role or colleagueship as primary;

- monitor this relationship through supervision and oversight and spiritual direction; and
- be transparent.

Dual relationships are not automatically wrong but the responsibility for keeping them healthy lies with the minister or the senior colleague/team leader, and these relationships need to be paid attention. Dual relationships can be inappropriate and dangerous because they can lead to impaired judgement and potential conflicts of interest, and can lead to exploitation of the vulnerable (which could be you). Attention needs to be paid to the health of a team and its internal dynamic or psychodrama. We cannot and should not expect those we minister to or work alongside to meet our personal needs. In our hierarchy of interests we must put those we care for or with alongside ahead of ourselves.

Assessment of Risk

Most of the time, ministers find that their misuse of a relationship with a church member or colleague did not grow out of some malicious intent or unresolved psychological issues. Rather, the violation occurred because they were unaware of their own personal needs and the church member or colleague was conveniently available to answer those needs. Using him or her to answer those needs made their life easier. Within this reality, ministers begin to grasp how they used their greater power in the relationship to cross the boundary and take what they needed from the church member or colleague.

Clearly violations of these boundaries falsify the covenantal relationship we have with the other. To understand why we cross boundaries, we have to examine the rationalizations that we use to disregard limits. Perhaps we convince ourselves that the pastoral or working relationship is over, or our behaviour isn't interfering with the ultimate aims of the pastoral or working relationship, or that we are behaving in a way other ministers or colleagues do. Rationalizations like this allow us to avoid facing the responsibility that we have to find acceptable alternatives. What can really convince us to cross the boundaries of a pastoral or working relationship is that we have either minimized the relationship or equalized the power differential by ignoring the reality of the working relationship. Maturing into taking responsibility for the maintenance of appropriate boundaries, and accepting that our pastoral relationships and working relationships with colleagues are not peer relationships, is to take the power and due authority our role and function gives us. We have also to accept that we can influence others by who we are, what we do and how we do it. We have already referred to Rollo May's [18] developed schema that can be useful in assessing our use of power. He places the exercise of power along a continuum that shows how power can be used to oppress or to expand another's freedom. His range of categories of power begins with exploitative power, and moves to manipulative power, competitive power, nutrient power and integrative power. For May, power can be used to liberate and empower those we work with and alongside or can be used to manipulate and bully.

Clearly we would wish to hold up the criterion of justice through liberation as a proper measure of our use of power. To assess our use of power we should ask is liberation and flourishing of another being achieved? Power is used rightly if it enables the other to be increasingly free, and used unfairly if it oppresses and bullies others into submission. It may only occur to us that we are using our personal power inappropriately if we receive feedback (often unsolicited) that this has been someone's experience of us. Our ministry and leadership will be healthier if we receive regular feedback that we have solicited or which has been solicited for us as part of a regular annual review. This is why I commend a programme of formal structured supervision of practice for all ministers and lay people involved in significant pastoral work in the life of the Church with a level of frequency and a robust system of recording as one means to review practice and behaviour. I am not suggesting such a system will produce perfection of practice or some kind of utopia. A real flesh and blood ministry among real flesh and blood people, and working colleagues who are not yet perfect demands much of us – and we are not (yet) perfect. I am reminded of Graham Greene's decrepit whisky priest[19] who sees Christ's resurrection as something dark and threatening, a terror and a demand from which we try to protect ourselves:

> 'Oh, the priest said, that's another thing altogether – God *is* love ... We wouldn't recognize *that* love. It might even look like hate. It would be enough to scare us – God's love. It set fire to a bush in the desert, didn't it, and smashed open graves and set the dead walking in the dark. Oh, a man like me would run a mile to get away if he felt that love around.'

In the incarnation we trust that in Christ Jesus, all that we are in our imperfections is assumed and healed, redeemed and restored by God. The Church brought to birth from the cross of Christ is marked by the wounds of that passion as well as by the joy of the gospel and exists not for itself but for the sake of the world, the redeemed world, the new community of grace and reconciliation.

This leads me to wonder how we model our ability to deal with mistakes, failure and wounds openly. Is honest acknowledgement of our capacity for sin and failure possible in ministry teams and in the wider life of the Church? Or are we too well defended to consider apology, where appropriate, an important ministry skill and a required skill for those who work together in teams? I am interested that many person-centred professions, such as doctors, are quicker to issue apologies for omissions than the Church is, despite our practice of regularly confessing our sins and failures in prayer and worship.

Marilynne Robinson in her novel *Gilead* offers a tantalizing and poignant image of the wayward son unable to find the restoration back into his father's home, society or the faith he so desires. In a significant episode, Jack (the prodigal son returned to the family home) begins a conversation about the nature of divine grace and forgiveness and the human capacity for change and transformation. He asks of his father and his father's friend, 'Are there people who are simply born evil, live evil lives, and then go to hell?' The two fathers, who are both ministers, fail to hear Jack's clear cry for help, his need to hear the affirmation of forgiveness, for words of welcome and acceptance. It takes Lila Ames, a woman whose voice is heard little in this novel though she appears in a later novel by Robinson, whose own past is kept shadowy and unexplored, whose faith is young and tender, to speak the words of absolution Jack longs to hear. It is she who says to Jack, 'A person can change. Everything can change.'[20]

Taking Responsibility

Change and transformation of our attitudes to others and our behaviours are possible, but they can take time and we need to be intentional about wanting to change and develop. We can learn what our preferences are in relation to work and ministry and become familiar enough with what our default positions are likely to be so that we and those who work with us can be aware of these and understand them when we present this way. Patient mapping of progress and affirmation from those who are witnesses to change, as well as suggestions for possible strategies to try out in order that we do not only and always default to our preferences, is important. Formal supervision can provide a suitable safe space to explore this kind of development of the adoption of a wider range of options and interventions. The ability to move between a number of different kinds of intervention styles in our dealings with others can be helpful in avoiding a limited and predictable response to presenting issues. We have already suggested paying some attention to John Heron's categories of intervention[21] because this can produce a greater degree of insight in those whose roles demand that they intervene regularly in the conduct of others. While we can only take responsibility for changes in our own behaviours and attitudes, we can work to ensure that those who work in proximity with us, and whose work we are responsible for, are able to receive a broad range of interventions from us. Heron's framework provides a model for analysing how support and challenge to team members or those we work with or minister to can be effectively and positively delivered. Heron's model has two basic styles – 'authoritative' and 'facilitative' – which further break down into six categories to describe how people intervene when supporting and challenging. If a supportive intervention is 'authoritative', it means that the responsible person 'supporting' is giving information, challenging the other person or suggesting what the other person should do. If a supporting intervention is 'facilitative', it means that the person 'helping' is drawing out ideas, solutions, self-confidence, and so on, from the other person, helping him or her to reach his or her own solutions or decisions.

Authoritative Interventions might be:

- *Prescriptive* – You explicitly direct the person you are supporting by giving advice and direction.
- *Informative* – You provide information to instruct and guide the other person.
- *Confronting* – You challenge the other person's behaviour or attitude. This style of intervention should not to be confused with aggressive confrontation. 'Confronting' in this scheme is positive and constructive. It helps the other person consider behaviour and attitudes of which they would otherwise be unaware. It is direct feedback.

Facilitative Interventions might be:

- *Cathartic* – You help the other person to express and overcome thoughts or emotions that they have not previously confronted.
- *Catalytic* – You help the other person reflect, discover and learn for him or herself. This helps him or her become more self-directed in making decisions, solving problems and so on.
- *Supportive* – You build up the confidence of the other person by focusing on their competences, qualities and achievements.

I have found Heron's insights both revealing and helpful when working in the world of ministerial formation with ordinands and students and in senior leadership in the church. Caring enough about someone to make a timely intervention is at the heart of attentiveness. Creating a range of interventions beyond our preferred or default modes is a very helpful skill in leadership. Left to our own devices we will often oscillate between being too directive or too supportive and not being sufficiently challenging. St Francis is reputed to have said that the best criticism of the bad is practice of the better, and I would suggest that working at suitable and careful interventions is the best way of taking someone's practice seriously, and that an appropriately chosen and executed intervention is a demonstration of real care. If we are convinced that we are first of all disciples and learners then the foundation on which we build is our Christian character, and every ordained minister is someone in whom a core identity of a disciple and follower of Christ is recognizable to others. The establishing of our core identities as human beings, as disciples and as ordained ministers takes time – we are not born mature and fully formed but slowly become so. Richard Rohr notes in his insightful exploration of what he describes as 'the second half of life':

First there is the fall, and then we recover from the fall. Both are the mercy of God.[22]

This is not for Rohr a necessarily chronological second half but rather a further, deeper journey which involves challenge, mistakes, failure, suffering and loss of control which lead to broader horizons and more mature understanding of the nature of God and humanity. Rohr explores whether we can learn to be generative persons who know an abundance of the presence of God and can share it generously with others from a strong conviction of the spaciousness of God. This spaciousness is not 'out there' but within, and so no despair of ours about the sadness and sorrow of the world can alter the reality of what we know to be true; that God so loved the world and gave himself for the world. When we give consideration as a Church as to who is most suitable to supervise the ministerial practice of others, it may well be those who can live in this very spaciousness because of their knowledge of weakness, failure, suffering and pain and who bring qualities of stillness and careful listening into this work, that we need to identify and resource to take on this work.

I have become interested in the theme of spiritual maturity and growth and how this impacts on, informs and transforms our ministerial practice. I see the Church has at times in the past catastrophically moved ministers around with insufficient intervention work offered in their practice and behaviour in order that change and growth might be encouraged or facilitated in them or indeed expected from them. A phrase I have used to describe this pattern of moving ministers from one appointment to another without appropriate intervention is 'zeroing'. Each time the minister moves to a new appointment without addressing the reasons why the previous appointment was problematic in terms of behaviours and attitudes, we turn back the clock to zero on their and our understanding of what went wrong and thus what needs addressing is ignored. The expectation that growth in a person might occur suggests an understanding that human beings can change and grow, that maturity is something to aim for and that good quality supervision of practice can lead us into change and transformation, not just of our practice but our development as human beings before God, who expect God to act in them, through them and with them. This is, for me, connected with our understanding of what we mean by vocation. The primary call is to humanity and to discipleship. For some people this then also becomes a call to ordained ministry. These 'callings', this vocation, needs to be mutually informing. I meet ministers who have adopted a professional persona or mask, a false self, and minister not through their humanity and because of their discipleship but from a distorted understanding of what ordained ministry requires. There is often a failure to recognize their humanity and continued discipleship, which can lead to others not recognizing their humanity or receiving their discipleship of Christ or seeing anything of the love and mercy of God in them.

Maturity is the outcome of a development process. We are called as human beings to grow constantly and continually into maturity, to be present to and interact with life experiences in such a way that, as long as we are alive, we are never finished with the process of becoming more integrated and more whole. I wonder what the distinctiveness of this process is for the Christian person, disciple and ordained minister.

Christian Maturity

Christian maturity must be Gospel-centred. We belong to a culture that praises self realization, speaks about finding oneself and about instant gratification of the desires of the self – and says we can buy products or earn them 'because you're worth it'. In contrast, entering into a journey towards maturity as a Christian necessitates becoming and remaining centred in Gospel values and imperatives. Values of compassion, solidarity, service, truth-telling, holding an option for the poor and marginalized, openness and willingness to transformation, willingness to release – even die to – that which is not life-giving and that which keeps us from recognizing and building up God's reign. So a real test for the ordained ministry of any Church is how it uses power. Does it speak words of humility while playing power games with others? What integrity is there? Surrender has become a dirty word in the Church or at least one viewed with suspicion. I have been vocal in the past in my own feminist critique of an over-emphasis in Christianity of surrendering the self with subsequent submission. But I am also clear that you can only surrender your will if you do so volitionally. If you don't offer up your own surrender it is isn't surrender, it is oppression.

Christian maturity is discipleship-centred. Christian discipleship must first be about being with Jesus, about entering into an intimate relationship with him, and then about following Jesus – even when that means staying behind him, letting him lead and accepting to go where he leads. Our commitment to discipleship may turn on what it means for us to follow Jesus and where the Spirit leads, rather than taking the lead ourselves. We need constantly to be reminded that the New Testament has little to say of leadership and much more to say about loving service (*diakonia*). Commitment to discipleship means following the poor, chaste, humble, challenging, terrifying Jesus of Nazareth, not some gooey statuette of a plaster Jesus. We belong to an idolatrous age – the idols we make are sometimes not just celebrities but about preservation of a way of life and the search for certainty. These shift our focus and deflect us from the demands of gospel discipleship.

Christian maturity must be relation-centred. Jesus' power, the power so unsettling and threatening to many of his contemporaries, especially to those in leadership, is relational power, the horizontal power of interaction among equally valued children of God rather than the hierarchical power which attempts to rank order the goodness of God's creation. This relational power nurtures others, empowers and affirms others, can be shared and indeed, on occasion, given away. Christian maturity requires that we foster healthy relationships in our lives, with ourselves, with others and with God. We need to have an ability to sustain intimate relationships that are honest, non-manipulative and non-judgemental; we need a capacity to love specific people, with their frailties and struggles, rather than loving abstract 'humanity' or God's people; an ability in the words of one writer, Ronald Rolheiser, 'to give oneself over to community, friendship, service, creativity, humour, delight, sacrifice, even martyrdom, in order to bring life into the world'.[23] An intimate relationship, a friendship with Christ is the essential foundation for a mature, adult life of faith, discipleship and effective, collaborative leadership in the Christian community. Relation-centred Christian living demands a we-consciousness that will be counter-cultural to the I-consciousness, which is often promoted in our culture. We need to ask with Sue Monk Kidd[24] how big is our "We"? Who is included within its embrace? How broadly do we measure the impact of our choices, actions and inactions?

Christian maturity involves a willingness to see (or attend) clearly. As Christians we aim towards a willingness to have our eyes opened to the reality around us, to see beyond and through the filters imposed by culture and society, to begin seeing through a gospel filter. Jon Sobrino speaks about 'culpable blindness'[25] to describe the problem of not wanting to see reality as it truly is, which leads to a falsification of reality and, existentially, to a self-interested way of understanding reality. Such an assessment makes selfish immaturity the dream state, and loving others generously the waking life. A mature willingness to see clearly opens us, inevitably, to the discomfort of realizing our own contributions to current reality and to the implicit question of whether we will take up our responsibility to respond in a way that will bring reality into closer alignment with gospel values. This is not a small challenge in our current world, in which so often people are intentionally presented with versions of reality that keep them unable to see its more troubling aspects, those that would most urgently cry out for attention, outrage and change. Christian maturity calls us to take responsibility for determining whether what we are handed as 'reality' actually corresponds to the whole of reality, and for renouncing a passivity that allows us not to see and allows our voices to remain silent.

Fostering Christian Maturity

What are some attitudes and practices we can cultivate in our ministers in order to move further along the way of the type of Christian maturity just described? I am committed to movement, progression and growth. I find the capacity for changing my understanding with a spiritual director, a loving community of friends and those who provide me with wise counsel, and within formal supervision of my ministerial practice that after 30 years of ordained ministry I still want and need. In public ministry we need to make a commitment to healing and growth, beginning with ourselves, and moving out into the world around us. A commitment to going inwards to do the necessary personal work involves identifying and healing (to the extent that this is possible) the wounded, blocked places that keep us bound in many ways. Doing this interior work then allows us to move outward as agents of healing, growth and transformation for our communities and churches and societies. Rather than being an introspective navel gazing, this invitation to be courageous and look within ourselves at what needs healing, at what unacknowledged motivations and hidden influences we might be carrying, allows us to offer ourselves more completely in being available to others as effective instruments of God's love and God's desire continuously to make all things new. Our theology of the Holy Spirit should see the third person of the Trinity as present in creation and active in constant re-creation. We celebrate that God looked on creation and saw that it was very good. We know that a well-developed person needs both boundaries and space. If we are offered no bounds or limits we become confused. If we are not given space to grow we will not achieve maturity but remain infantile. We need space and time to play and grow, and spaciousness is limited in a frantically busy Church taking refuge from anxiety by doing more and more. Self-confrontation is a painful, yet essential, part of maturing – both psychologically and spiritually. Growth into both spiritual and psychological maturity is always connected to painful processes of 'purification'. In the *Narnia Chronicles* Eustace Clarence Scrubb, who was a boy and becomes a dragon, is baptized in a pool of purifying water and sheds his outer layers of tough hide. Because we know it may be a painful process we resist embarking on such a journey, preferring to stay where we are, more or less comfortably settled into life, and sometimes covered in a thick hide obscuring our true selves, but forfeiting the opportunities to be stretched into fully becoming the people God made us to be as mature adult Christians. We prefer a cocooned and swaddled infancy.

In maturing we need to move from unconscious to conscious loving. The gospel narrative makes it clear that the Christian way – the mature Christian way – consists in loving. Difficult as it is for us, the invitation is to learn to love as Jesus loved, with insight, compassion, sensitivity, justice and self-surrender. It is in the process of striving to love as Jesus did that God will make us whole – and that we will become mature Christians. Loving faithfully, loving as Jesus loved, is a coming-to-see process, in which we become conscious of the costs and realities of loving well, and in which we are able to move beyond the inevitable disappointments and disillusionments to a conscious choice and commitment to love because that has become the only 'way' that makes sense and gives life.[26]

We must also cultivate a capacity for and a commitment to complex thinking and analysis, with which to understand and address the challenges of our time. The capacity to think and analyse and reflect critically, and to wrestle with difficult things when questions are asked which demand personal and structural change, is an important aspect of personal growth and intellectual maturity. The task of maturing in faith and in ministry is an active process, requiring a safe space in which to do the work, skilled practitioners such as supervisors and spiritual directors who can accompany and enable the work, and an open-hearted approach by those brave enough to engage. Maturing is a significant element in our flourishing as human beings and as ministers. What the process of maturing becomes when we reflect about the nature of the Church is interesting – a state of non-anxious presence, focused on risk-taking and bold loving, a Church attentive to the work of the Spirit and fixed on Christ, a Church willing to follow where Jesus leads and not just concerned to worship God. Such a Church, capable of reverent uncertainty, would be fit to serve the present age which is fearful and anxious about so many things.

Notes

1 Parker J. Palmer, 2009, *A Hidden Wholeness: The Journey Toward an Undivided Life*, Hoboken, NJ: Jossey Bass.

2 Toni Cade Bambara, 1998, *The Salt Eaters*, London: Women's Press.

3 R. Meredith Belbin, 2010, *Team Roles at Work*, London: Routledge.

4 James Alison, 1993, *Knowing Jesus*, London: SPCK.

5 Sara Savage and Eolene Boyd-Macmillan, 2007, *The Human Face of Church*, Norwich: Canterbury Press.

6 Richard Gula, 1995, *Ethics in Pastoral Ministry*, Mahwah, NJ: Paulist Press, p. 29.

7 John Macmurray, 1961, *Persons in Relation*, London: Faber & Faber.

8 Stephen Pickard, *Theological Foundations for Collaborative Ministry*, Ashgate, 2009.

9 Pickard, p. 17. Pickard is drawing on the work of Robert Hannaford in making this point.

10 Pickard, p. 43.

11 Pickard, p. 229.

12 Tom Smail, 1995, *Charismatic Renewal*, London: SPCK.

13 Rowan Williams, 2004, *Silence and Honeycakes*, Kidderminster: Lion Books, p. 22.

14 Williams, p. 24.

15 Annie Dillard, 1984, *Teaching a Stone to Talk: Expeditions and Encounters,* New York: Harper and Row.
16 Williams, p. 5.
17 Richard Gula, 2010, *Just Ministry: Professional Ethics for Clergy,* Mahwah, NJ: Paulist Press, p. 74.
18 Rollo May, 1971, *Power and Innocence,* London: W. W. Norton.
19 Graham Greene, 2015, *The Power and the Glory,* London: Penguin Random House.
20 Marilynne Robinson, 2005, *Gilead,* London: Virago.
21 John Heron, *Intervening in Human Relations: An Introduction to John Heron's Six Category Intervention Analysis,* Leeds: Oasis Press.
22 Richard Rohr, 2012 *Falling Upward,* p.vi, London: SPCK.
23 Ronald Rolheiser, 1999, *The Holy Longing,* New York: Doubleday.
24 Sue Monk Kidd, 2002, *The Secret Life of Bees,* New York: Viking.
25 Jon Sobrino, 2004, *Where is God? Earthquake, Terrorism, Barbarity and Hope,* New York: Orbis Books.
26 Wilkie Au and Noreen Cannon, 1995, *Urgings of the Heart: A Spirituality of Integration,* Mahwah, NJ: Paulist Press.

5

A Supervised Ministry

We begin this final chapter by considering why the formal one-to-one supervision of ministers might be particularly pertinent, important and significant at this point in the Church's life, and why we might commend it as a significant tool of accountability and oversight within the Church alongside other means of personal and organizational accountability, such as spiritual direction, coaching and mentoring, ministry team and staff meetings, Synods and other expressions of ministerial collegiality. In 2015 the Methodist Church issued a public apology to survivors/victims of sexual abuse whose experiences had emerged in a review of past cases of the safeguarding of children and vulnerable adults in the Methodist Church from 1950 to 2014.

The (then) Secretary of the Conference, the Reverend Dr Martyn Atkins, offered this apology:

> On behalf of the Methodist Church in Britain I want to express an unreserved apology for the failure of its current and earlier processes fully to protect children, young people and adults from physical and sexual abuse inflicted by some ministers. The abuse that has been inflicted by some Methodists on children, young people and adults is, and will remain, a deep source of grief and shame to the Church.
>
> We have not always listened properly to those abused or cared for them, and this is deeply regrettable. In respect of these things we have, as a Christian Church, clearly failed to live in ways that glorify God and honour Christ.

> I am certain that the Methodist Conference will want to resolve to do all in its power to improve its systems to protect children, young people and adults from abuse within the life of the Church and on Church premises, and to review them diligently on a regular basis.

This independent Past Cases Review considered all safeguarding cases for which there were written records and those recalled from memory by ministers and members of the Church going back to 1950. These included cases that occurred within a church context as well as those which were reported to the Church as a matter of pastoral concern but which occurred away from the church.

In each identified case, the Church's response was reviewed as to whether it had been safe, pastorally appropriate and compliant with current legislation and policy. Where possible and appropriate, cases were referred to the police, or other remedial action was taken. The aim of conducting the review and writing the report was to learn the lessons of the past so that safeguarding work within the Methodist Church would be of the highest possible standard and the Church a safer place for all.

The review identified 1,885 past cases, which included sexual, physical, emotional and domestic abuse as well as cases of neglect. In approximately one quarter of these cases, church ministers or lay employees were identified as the perpetrators or alleged perpetrators. In 61 of these cases there was contact with the police and there were ongoing police investigations as a result of the Report. The review, which lasted more than three years, was led by former Deputy Chief Executive of Barnardo's, Jane Stacey, who had a long career in senior management of organizations in the child welfare field. As the Report was published she stated that:

> It was a courageous act for the Methodist Church to launch such a comprehensive Past Cases Review. Even more courageous was the response from the survivors or victims who

relived very difficult experiences to contribute to the review, either directly or through a third party. However thorough the review has been, there are undoubtedly cases that have not been reported and the Church would encourage survivors and victims and those with any further information to contact the Safeguarding Team.

Jane Stacey's encouragement was heard and her assurance that survivors would be listened to and support offered was believed. Publication of the Report titled *Courage, Cost and Hope* in 2015 resulted in further cases being reported, as survivors found the courage to report their abuse. In 2015 Jane Stacey noted:

> There are many lessons to be learnt, but the most challenging are those that require a significant culture change throughout the church, and particularly for ministers and church leaders. The Church will need further courage to implement the review's recommendations, which are far-reaching and call for major changes in both practice and culture. The Methodist Church has already taken measures to improve safeguarding across the Connexion and implementing the learning from this review will be the next step to ensuring that the Church can be a safe place for all.

The Methodist Conference of 2015 received the report of the Past Cases Review, *Courage, Cost and Hope*, and its 23 recommendations were accepted.[1]

Significantly, a case was made in the Past Cases Review report for formal one-to-one supervision for all ministers and their ministerial practice as being an important tool for addressing the weakness identified in the Methodist Church in relation to support and accountability for safe ministerial practice, with reference to a study of the Child Exploitation and Online Protection Centre (CEOP):

Studies have demonstrated that one of the most effective safeguards within organizations or professional settings is to provide frequent, open and supportive supervision of staff.

The Past Cases Review report went on to acknowledge the differences between the Church and other organizations (notably for the Methodist Church that its clergy are not employees but rather in a lifelong covenant relationship with the Conference), nevertheless noting that it was difficult to see why the evidence from such studies should not apply to the Church. It is also noteworthy that the CEOP study specifically included religious organizations.[2] The recommendation was that the first group to be appointed supervisors and to enter into formal one-to-one supervision were the senior leaders, the 32 Chairs of the Districts.

At no point does the 2015 report suggest that supervision is the great panacea which will remove all risk from ministerial practice. Rather there is a strong emphasis in the Past Cases Review Report of the significant contribution that formal one-to-one supervision of practice might offer as one tool of accountability alongside others. It is noteworthy that in the hearings of the Independent Inquiry into Child Sexual Abuse, a question was raised as to why clergy were not formally supervised in their pastoral practice. Another tool of accountability within the recommendations of the report was the suggestion that a Code of Conduct for clergy might be developed. It was suggested that such a Code might contribute significantly to a change of culture in the life of the Church from clergy who operate in isolated and lonely ways, which make them and others vulnerable, to a clergy who are more accountable, are supported and challenged and so are safer in their practice. It is yet to be demonstrated that laying out clearly expectations of conduct will, of itself, increase the quality of conduct in ministers, but it may well at least raise levels of awareness of what others regard as minimum standards of conduct.

It is vital when considering developments in tools of accountability to acknowledge that the awareness of a need for greater accountability and reduction of risk in ministerial practice is not new in the Methodist Church, but rather a continuous flowing strand of expectation and high standards. The Past Cases Review provided a particular and sharp focus on the conduct of lay and ordained persons in one denomination over a 50-year timeframe, but not a new or previously unexplored one. The Methodist Church, along with its ecumenical partners, is clear that offering formal supervision of practice to ministers is a good thing, and has been assiduous in ensuring that probationer ministers in their early years of ministry should receive a healthy combination of support and challenge through supervision in order to inculcate good practice in terms of accountability and reduction of risk. The Church has understood this both in terms of the vitally necessary protection of children and vulnerable adults from harm in order to create safer space in the Church, but also because ministerial health, well-being and flourishing is of great concern, and perhaps particularly at a time of reduction in ordained ministerial resources. A report to the Methodist Council regarding proposals for an Interim Supervision policy for ministers in the Methodist Church suggests:

> Structured supervision is also [offered] for the sake of supported, reflective practice that is able to identify emerging challenges [in mission] and discern strategies to address them within the horizon of God's justice and love and within the purposes of the Methodist Church.[3]

This is a bold claim for the value of supervision as a missional tool and one that is worth further reflection. It is interesting to note that this suggestion that supervision might be a key tool by which the Methodist Church could become a more effective agent in God's mission can be traced in a number of earlier pieces of reflection on mission and ministry in the Methodist Church. In 2002 in a report entitled *What is a Presbyter?*, this perspective was expressed as a more mutual expression of shared accountability:

A SUPERVISED MINISTRY

> At the same time all Methodist ministers who are ordained and in full connexion are called to respond wherever they are most required (in the collective view of the Church expressed through the Conference) to meet those same needs. They are therefore deployed as individuals to enact this collegial responsibility. To this end they are all stationed by the Conference. Some are stationed within particular appointments, others without appointment or with permission to study. Wherever possible they are all linked together with other ministers in teams for mutual supervision and support.[4]

The Methodist Church in previous explorations of accountability has stated that all its ministers (presbyters and deacons) are accountable for their ministry

- to God;
- to the Church – through a 'covenant relationship' with the Conference in which a presbyter or deacon accepts the authority and support of the Conference and is in turn entrusted with representing them to others;
- to ordained colleagues – through 'watching over each other in love' communally and collegially in ad hoc relationships and groups, staff meetings, Ministerial (sic) Sessions of Synod, and the Ministerial (sic) Session of Conference[5] and for deacons through the Convocation; and
- to others – through behaving with integrity, competence and according to the best standards of practice towards those to whom she or he ministers.[6]

In a 2005 Conference Report entitled *What is a Circuit Superintendent?*, it was noted that:

> Superintendents exercise their share of that general collective role, but within it they also have particular responsibilities:
>
>> They are expected to gather together any presbyters and any deacons appointed to or stationed in the circuit, and

any lay workers employed in the circuit *in order for them to take prayerful counsel together, support each other, supervise each other in their professional practice and develop vision*. As such the Superintendents do not just (in the words of Standing Order 700 (9)) 'have oversight of all the ministers, deacons and probationers stationed in the Circuit' but also allow themselves to be 'watched over in love' in turn by them. In all this they are taking the lead in a group which is primarily exercising *leadership*.[7] [my italics]

In 2008 in a Conference report entitled *With Integrity and Skill*, addressing issues of confidentiality in the life of the Church, it was stated that:

> There can be tension between those in the Church convinced of a need to be more 'professional', including the introduction of job descriptions for clergy and lay workers, supervision, quality assurance and accountable appraisal, and those who believe the Church to be a different kind of organization. There need not be a clash between the 'professional' view and the 'covenantal' view. Regardless of personal preference about which perspective is most appropriate in a Christian pastoral context, the need for good practice and appropriate boundaries remains the same. *This report recommends the use of supervision for those who offer pastoral care – lay, ordained, paid and voluntary – and suggests a range of models to choose from.* [my italics]

The report recommended that all those in a recognized pastoral relationship be supported through a structure of formal reflective practice (called 'supervision') and that work be done to bring such a system into effect and to make this compulsory for presbyters, deacons and lay workers with pastoral responsibilities.[8]

We would also want to acknowledge that from the very beginning of Methodism, Mr Wesley's supervision of his assistants was formal, in a one-to-one format as well as in a small group and clearly used as a means of accountability. This collegial responsibility also maintains one of the original emphases of the body of Mr Wesley's preachers and helpers, which eventually developed into the body of Methodist Ministers (Presbyters), namely that of being something like a religious order. The inscription in the copy of the Large Minutes, and the successor to them given in the late eighteenth, nineteenth and early twentieth centuries to all those preachers and helpers who were received into Full Connexion with the Conference, said, 'As long as you freely consent to, and earnestly endeavour to walk by, these Rules, we shall rejoice to acknowledge you as a fellow-labourer' (note 20).[9] Brian Beck notes this is hardly a take-it-or-leave-it approach but rather a take it or leave us approach.[10]

Methodism has then, from the beginning, emphasized mutual and collegial accountability, the value of regular staff meetings and a willingness to engage with issues of practice and behaviour. This theme of accountability is not a recent response to contemporary issues but rather a core value of Methodism and a key element in Methodist ministerial practice. When Jane Stacey in 2015 called for a culture change in Methodism, in order that the Church be a safe place for all, she was, in fact, issuing a call and invitation to return to a culture of accountability which was always a feature of Methodism, but which had been eroded in some places and to some extent where individualism had been unchecked.

I am confident that formal one-to-one supervision of one minister by another, and supported by an agreed written record, is a feature of ministerial practice that John Wesley would recognize, approve and participate in fully as a scheme. I think it certain that he would prefer to supervise than be supervised, but nevertheless from the beginnings of the Holy Club at Oxford, to the first classes, bands and the Methodist Societies, the purpose of being present to one another in this way which he urged upon the people called Methodists was to support one another in the pursuit of holiness of heart and life, which means eternal and generous love filling the heart and governing the life. Such methods were commended to every disciple and a further layer of accountability was present in the Rules for members of the societies[11] and 'The 12 Rules of a Helper'.[12]

For Wesley, a heart overflowing with God's love was always represented by a governed and disciplined and ordered life. There is a consistency therefore in the Methodist Church, in the early part of the twenty-first century, moving from issuing a public apology for failures of safeguarding children and vulnerable adults in the past to enacting a commitment to culture change in the life of Church expressed in a scheme to ensure formal one-to-one supervision of its ministers as means to improve accountability. Such an implementation as part of culture change in the Church is costly in terms of training of ministers in supervision and in allocation of resources, and is both demanding and time-consuming as a regular commitment, particularly for Circuit Superintendents, depending on the size of the Circuit team of lay and ordained staff. Methodist Districts and Circuits vary significantly in size and great care is required to develop a system of formal supervision that can be sustained over the full length of an appointment and in every context. The effort required to implement this particular recommendation of the Past Cases Review is, I believe, worthwhile because of the potential it holds to reduce ministerial isolation and create a more fully accountable ministry and Church. Such an effort, after all, is an expression of the Church seeking to fulfil its calling to be salt and light, to be a holy people, and such an effort is worth engaging with. The Church exists to reflect the love of God in Christ, to offer bread and not a stone to those who come to the Church and to those who serve it, in order that we all might live abundantly and flourish richly, in order that the world might be transformed.

Notes

1 See Appendix p. 116.
2 Past Cases Review, *Courage, Cost and Hope*, 2015, section H.1.9, Report to the Methodist Conference, www.methodist. org.uk.
3 MC/17/46 Supervision Policy 2.2, www.methodist.org.uk.
4 *What is a Presbyter?* 2002, Report to the Methodist Conference, www.methodist.org.uk.
5 Since this Report was written the term Ministers is now retained to refer to both presbyters and deacons. These sessions of the Synod and the Conference are now described as the Presbyteral Session.
6 *The Nature of Oversight*, 2005, Report to the Methodist Conference, www.methodist.org.uk.
7 *What is a Circuit Superintendent?*, 2005, Report to the Methodist Conference, www.methodist.org.uk.
8 *With Integrity and Skill*, 2008, Report to the Methodist Conference, www.methodist.org.uk.
9 *The Theology of Pastoral Care*, 2011, Report to the Methodist Conference, www.methodist.org.uk.
10 Brian E. Beck, 2018, *Methodist Heritage & Identity*, Abingdon: Routledge.
11 The Wesley's '*Rules of the Society*', 1743, The Constitutional Practice and Discipline of the Methodist Church, Vol.1, Peterborough, MPH.
12 '*The 12 Rules of a Helper*', 1753, Constitutional Practice, Vol. 1, Peterborough, MPH.

Appendix

The recommendations of the Past Cases Review Report, *Courage, Cost and Hope*, were as follows:

R1 That an Implementation Group be established to oversee the implementation of all the PCR's recommendations that are agreed by the Conference and that membership of this group be agreed by the Conference.

R2 That selection criteria for district Chairs, the Warden of the MDO and members of the SLG of the Connexional team include awareness of and ability to deal effectively with safeguarding issues.

R3 That policy and guidance be provided to define what should be recorded by ministers or others undertaking pastoral work and that this be clear about requirements for each specific role as well as providing guidance for best practice.

R4 That policy and guidance be provided about storage and access to pastoral records, specifying particularly requirements on ministerial handover.

R5 That all people who deliver safeguarding training at Foundation or Leadership Module be required to attend training on the findings of the Past Cases Review.

APPENDIX

R6 That the findings from the PCR be incorporated into the training of ministers irrespective of the pathway they are following.

R7 That a system of structured supervision for ministers be instituted to address the identified weakness in relation to accountability and support in terms of safe practice. The urgency of this requirement is recognized but also the capacity/skills/resource issues that are raised. Ideally the timescales would be as follows:

- A draft supervision policy is produced by a working party that has the skills/knowledge to reflect the relevant dimensions of accountability and important theological underpinning. The draft policy to be considered by the Methodist Council in October 2015.
- A training course for supervisors to be developed by the end of December 2015.
- A pilot roll-out of supervision across 2 Districts is undertaken for 12 months (January-December 2016) starting with the training of supervisors in January/February and supervision sessions starting in March 2016.
- A report on the pilot to be presented to Methodist Council in October 2016 with recommendations for a roll-out across the Connexion to start in January 2017.

It is however recognized that as such timescales have resource implications, the Implementation Group should meet as soon as possible following the Conference, to agree a timetable and secure the required resources.

R8 That serious consideration be given to producing a Code of Conduct for ministers along the lines of that produced by the Church of England.

R9 That, until the Methodist Church has robust accountability processes in place and fully operational, an annual independent audit of progress on these culture change recommendations and in particular on the mainstreaming of safeguarding awareness be carried out: and that a framework for the audits and proposals on who should carry them out be agreed by the Methodist Council in October 2015.

R10 Training: that the pattern of training for members of the Connexional Complaints Panel continue to be developed so as to ensure: an annual training event; that all members of the Panel undertake both the Foundation and the Leadership module; that additional sections of the Leadership module be prepared to cover the impact of abuse on victims, pattern/models of abuse and risk management in the Church; and that, when developed, these sections be required training for those hearing complaints relating to a safeguarding concern.

R11 That the Past Cases Review definition of a 'Safeguarding concern' be used by Local Complaints Officers, Complaints Teams and Discipline Committees.

R12 That work be undertaken to ensure that a rigorous system of liaison and consultation between all parts of the complaints process, the resignation [of ministers] process, suspensions, and the Connexional Safeguarding Officer to ensure that appropriate advice is obtained on cases that contain a safeguarding concern or sexual harassment.

R13 That work be undertaken to develop further best practice guidance including, but not limited to, guidance on appropriate communication with complainants and respondents; guidance on the choice of venues for meetings and hearings; and guidance on questioning of complainants and respondents.

APPENDIX

R14 Recording and monitoring: that a system be established to monitor the implementation of decisions of Discipline Committees (and where appropriate Complaints teams) and that their implementation be recorded.

R15 That, in the light of the learning points highlighted in section H.3 of the full report, all current safeguarding training materials be reviewed and that, specifically, further sections be added to the Leadership module, using anonymized case material from the PCR.

R16 That the roles that are required to attend training at which level are reviewed.

R17 That the appropriate bodies consider developing materials to promote wider awareness of safe relationships within church communities.

R18 That, in the light of the learning from section H.3 and H.1 of the full report, the Safeguarding Policy and other relevant policies be reviewed and amended.

R19 That, a connexional register of Covenants of Care be established and held by the Connexional Safeguarding Team in order to promote effective and consistent monitoring of those who might pose a risk; and that this register include those who have requested to worship under such arrangements but not followed through; and that policies be developed to ensure that all sharing of information is justified and safe.

R20 That all reviews and amendments to policies and training material involve consultation with victims/survivors.

R21 That the Connexional Safeguarding Team identify any further learning points emerging from their follow-up work and report them initially to the Implementation Group when the PCR-related activity is completed, or by March 2016, whichever is the sooner.

R22 That the resources required for the Safeguarding Team to complete the PCR work as outlined in section 1 of the full report be agreed.

R23 That a Connexional resource be identified to support survivors/victims if District support is not appropriate/possible; and that resources be identified to support working with established survivor/victim groups.

Acknowledgement of Sources

The author and publisher are grateful for permission to use extracts under copyright from the following publications.

Patrick Kavanagh, 1972, 'The Hospital', *Collected Poems*, London: Martin, Brian and O'Keeffe Ltd, p. 153. Used by permission.

Denise Levertov, 2002, 'In Whom We Live and Move and Have Our Being', *Selected Poems of Denise Levertov*, New York: New Directions Publishing. Permission applied for.

Thomas Lux, 'Refrigerator, 1957', 1997, *New and Selected Poems, 1975–1995*. Copyright © 1997 by Thomas Lux. Reprinted by permission of Houghton Mifflin Harcourt Publishing Company. All rights reserved.

Derek Walcott, 1987, Love after Love', *Collected Poems 1948–84*, New York: Farrar, Straus and Giroux. Permission applied for.

Index of Names and Subjects

accountability 9, 27
  Code of Conduct for clergy 109
  collegial and corporate 30–1
  formal supervision 30–1
  Methodist Church and 44–7
  sexual abuse cases and 106–10
  structured supervision and 110–13
  to whom 111
Acts of the Apostles
  1.8 56
  11.30 36
  14.23 36
  15.22 36
  20.24 70
  20.28 29
Aelred of Rivaulx 29
Alexander, Loveday 60
Alison, James 78–9
  positive disruption 78–9
Alpha courses 67–6
Atkins, Rev. Dr Martyn 106–7
attending
  to Christ 62–3

Christian maturity 101–2
Church as witness 55–6
  embodying and pointing 56–7
  examples of 52–4
  faithful improvisation 58–60, 61
  to situations 65–9
  spiritual direction and 69–74
  witness and 55–65
Augustine of Hippo
  Confessions 11
  De trinitate 10–11

Bambara, Toni Cade 75
Beck, Brian 113
Belbin, Meredith 76
Bernard of Chartres 64
boundaries and limits 80–1
  Christian maturity 102–3
  colleagues and 89–95
  learning 17–21
  in ministry 43
  pastoral relationships 89–95
  relationship risks 92–5
  Winnicott and 17, 20
Boyd-Macmillan, Eolene 80

Burgess, Neil
Into Deep Waters 34–5

Caravaggio 22
change of attitudes 95–6
character
  expectations of ministry 13
  process of formation 12–17
Child Exploitation and
  Online Protection Centre
  (CEOP) 108–9
Child Sexual Abuse,
  Independent Inquiry into
  55
Christianity
  maturity 99–104
  overwhelming experience 4
Church of England
  clergy well-being 16–17
  safeguarding the vulnerable
  55
churches
  accountability to 111
  attending to the world 55–6
  expectations of ministry 13
  experience for ministry 5
  local witness 57–8
colleagues/team
  accountability to 111–12
  boundaries and 89–95
  common ground 86–9
  departures of 78
  difference and world views
  79–82
  dual relationships 91–2
  leaning towards others
  82–6
  married couples and 91
  teamwork/teambuilding
  77–82
  understanding and empathy
  for 75–7
community
  koinonia 86
  Trinitarian theology and
  83–6
Confessions (Augustine of
  Hippo) 11
connexionalism
  Methodist ordination and
  45–6
  Methodist understanding
  of 30
context, attention to 67–8
Corinthians, First Letter to
  1.22 84
Courage, Cost and Hope
  (Methodist report) 108,
  116–20
creativity 5

De trinitate (Augustine of
  Hippo) 10–11
Dillard, Annie 88
discipleship
  Christian maturity and 100
  learning and 61
  see also witness

Ellsworth, Elizabeth 17–28
Evagrius 52

Fisher, Peter
  Outside Eden 23–4

INDEX OF NAMES AND SUBJECTS

flexibility 5
Ford, David 4
formation, ministerial 3–4
  knowledge and 17–18
  potentiality and 21–2
  process of 12–17
  space and time for 17–21
St Francis 97

Galatians, Letter to
  6.2 85
Gilead (Robinson) 26–7
God
  formation and 16
  gracious love in Christ
    63–5
  guarding us 25
  spiritual direction 69–70
  transformation through
    10–12
Goncharov, Ivan
  Oblamov 26
Greene, Graham
  The Power and the Glory 94
Gula, Richard 10, 81

Hahn, Celia 8
Herbert, George 1
  'Love' 22
Heron, John 48, 96–7
Higton, Mike 60, 61
Holy Club 113
Holy Spirit
  agent of formation 16
  Christian maturity and 102
  covenant and church 37–8
  paschal model 84

honesty, self-examination
  and 9

identity, development of 19
imperfection, knowledge of
  24
improvisation
  deep learning and 61
  in witness 58–60, 61
'In Whom We Live and
  Move and Have Our
  Being' (Levertov) 24–5
inequality
  in power relationships 7–8
intervention
  authoritative or facilitative
    96–7
  practice of the better 97
  spiritual maturity 97–9
Isserlis, Stephen 65

Jamie, Kathleen
  Sightlines 52–3
Jeremiah
  18.1–4 14
Jesus Christ
  attending to 62–3
  bearing fruit and 25
  Christian maturity and 103
  context of followers 68
  disruption for disciples 78–9
  embodiment of 56–7
  Fisher on 'unfairness' of
    23–4
  God's gracious love in 63–5
  humble loving service of
    68–9

imitation of 80
mature discipleship 100
power and vulnerability 8
on service 6–7
shared ministry and 88
and the Syro-Phoenican
  woman 7
witness and 55–6
John, Gospel of
  10.17–18 7
  13.3–5 68
  15 25
  19.26–7 56
  19.30 84
  19.34–5 84
  20.31 56

Kavanagh, Patrick 31–2
Kidd, Sue Monk 101
knowledge of imperfection 24
Kristeva, Julia 33

Lane, Belden 54
  *The Solace of Fierce
    Landscapes* 52
Leach, Jane 71
leadership
  accountability and 112
  development of 22
  expectations for 13
learning
  boundaries and space for
    17–21
  improvisation and 61
Levertov, Denise
  'In Whom We Live' 24–5
Levinas, Emmanuel 33

Lewis, C. S.
  Narnia Chronicles 103
loneliness, ministry and 6
'Love' (Herbert) 22
'Love after Love' (Walcott)
  22–3
Lux, Thomas
  'Refrigerator' 66–7

Macmurray, John 81
Mahler, Gustav 65
Mandelson, Peter 58
Mark, Gospel of
  10.42–45 6–7
Mary, mother of Jesus
  at the empty tomb 38
  as our own 63
  at the tomb 16
Maslow, Abraham
  hierarchy of needs 1–2
Matthew, Gospel of
  15.21–28 7
  17.2 10
maturity
  Christian 99–104
  spiritual 97–9
May, Rollo
  power relations 93
  typology of power 8
Methodist Church
  accountability 44–7
  circuit staff 78
  Code of Conduct for
    ministers 16–17
  collegial accountability
    113–14
  connexion 30, 113

INDEX OF NAMES AND SUBJECTS

Courage, Cost and Hope
  report 108, 116–20
With Integrity and Skill
  report 112
MDR and 9–10, 49–50,
  73–4
network of oversight 34
the Ordinal 42–3
ordination service 72
oversight in 29
presbyters' covenant 11
safeguarding the vulnerable
  55
sexual abuse cases 106–10,
  114
Superintendent minister
  36–7
*What is a Circuit
  Superintendent?* report
  112
What is a Presbyter? report
  110
Methodist Formation 12
Miller-McLemore, Bonnie 47
Ministerial Development
  Review (MDR) 9–10
  risk management and
    recording 49–50
  spiritual direction and 73–4
ministry
  encompassment 24–7
  factors for flourishing 2–5
  impact on others 75–7
  limits and boundaries 43
  obligations of 30
  pastoral relationships 47–8,
    89–91

personality and 6
Priesthood of all Believers
  83
risk in relationships 92–5
in supervision 39
Moses the Black 87–8

Narnia Chronicles (Lewis)
  103
Nativities and Passions
  (Smith) 43
Neruda, Pablo 54
'no', saying 43–4

Oblamov (Goncharov) 26
ordination
  accountability and 44–7
  connexionalism and 45–6
  as a gift of the church 30
  liturgy of 42–3, 72
others
  accountability to 111
  awareness of 75–7
  difference and 79
  see also colleagues/team
Outside Eden (Fisher) 23–4
oversight
  definition of 29
  supervision and 36–7

pain, formative experience
  of 4
Palmer, Parker J. 75
pastoral care
  relationships 47–8, 89–91
  supervision and 38–9
Paterson, Michael 71

127

Paul
  be members of one another 84
  living by God's will 10
personality, introverts and extroverts 80
Pickard, Stephen
  Theological Foundation for Collaborative Ministry 82–4
play, improvisation 58
Pohly, Kenneth
  on formation 15
  transforming the rough places 37, 38
Il Postino (Skarmata) 54, 66
potentiality, formation and 21–2
power and authority 5 8
  Christian maturity and 100
  Jesus on service 6–7
  laying down 7
  pastoral relationships 89–91
  unequal relationships 7–8
The Power and the Glory (Greene) 94
The President of the Methodist Church v
Preston 45
Psalms, Book of
  23.5 and 6 60
  121 25

Queen's Foundation, Birmingham
  Methodist Formation and 12, 13–14

'Refrigerator' (Lux) 66
relationality
  ministry and personality 5–6
relationships
  boundaries and limits 89–95
  colleagues 91–2
  pastoral 47–8
  risk assessment and 92–5
  unequal 7–8
responsibility 102–3
risk assessment
  relationship boundaries 92–5
Robinson, Marilynne
  Gilead 26–7, 94–5
Rohr, Richard 97–8
Rolheiser, Ronald 101
Roman Catholic Church
  constitutive ministry 82
Romans, Letter to
  12.2 10

Savage, Sara 80
Schon, Donald 32
service, loving *(diakonia)* 29
sexual abuse cases
  official inquiry into 55
  Past Cases Review 106–10, 114
Sightlines (Jamie) 52–3
Skarmata, Antonio
  Il Postino 54, 66
Smail, Tom
  theology of Holy Spirit 84–5

INDEX OF NAMES AND SUBJECTS

Smith, Martin
  Nativities and Passions 43
Sobrino, Jon 101
society, current uncertainties and 2
The Solace of Fierce Landscapes (Lane) 52
Song of Songs
  gaze of the beloved 53–4
spiritual direction 69–74
  supervision and 71–4
  three strands of 70
Sri Lanka 59–60
Stacey, Jane 107–8, 113
stress and anxiety
  power relations and 7
supervision
  accountability and 109–14
  'bringing to birth' model 34–6
  characteristics of 38–40
  as covenental 37–8, 39
  definition of 29
  intentional 40
  learning and 32–3
  as ministry 39
  as overseeing 36–7
  Past Cases Review on 110
  pastoral care and 38–9, 89–91
  recording 49
  reflection and 39–40
  review of performance in 9–10
  risk management 49–50
  shared agenda model of 33, 40–2

spiritual direction 71–4
training in supervision 33
transformation and 37–8
using ministerial practices 45–8
Ward's model of 33–4
surrendering the self 100, 103

teamwork *see* colleagues/team
Theological Foundation for Collaborative Ministry (Pickard) 82–4
Thornton, Martin 69
Trinity
  relational theology of 83–6
  spiritual formation and 13

values
  Christian maturity 99
Volf, Miroslav
  identity and conflict 19–20

Walcott, Derek
  'Love after Love' 22–3
Ward, Frances 33–4
Watts, Isaac 69
Wells, Samuel 60
Wesley, John
  being in connexion 46
  God's love and order 114
  a strict account 9
  supervision and 112–13
What is a Circuit Superintendent? (Methodist report) 111–12

What is a Presbyter?
 (Methodist report) 110
Williams, Rowan
 manifestation of thoughts 88
 our neighbours 87–8
Winnicott, Donald
 boundaries and space 17, 20
 Ward and 33
With Integrity and Skill
 (Methodist report) 112

witness
 attending and 55–62
 communicating 65–6
 other witnesses and 63–5
 women spreading the word 55–6

Yannaras, Christos 53–4

Zweig, Stefan 47–8